The Social Anxiety and Shyness Solution

Learn How to Be Yourself and Talk to Anyone by Improving Your People & Conversation Skills to Influence & Win Friends (It's OK Not to Be Nice)

Dean J. Arquette

© Copyright 2019 - All rights reserved.

The content contained within this book may not be reproduced, duplicated or transmitted without direct written permission from the author or the publisher.

Under no circumstances will any blame or legal responsibility be held against the publisher, or author, for any damages, reparation, or monetary loss due to the information contained within this book. Either directly or indirectly.

Legal Notice

This book is copyright protected. This book is only for personal use. You cannot amend, distribute, sell, use, quote or paraphrase any part, or the content within this book, without the consent of the author or publisher.

Disclaimer Notice

Please note the information contained within this document is for educational and entertainment purposes only. All effort has been executed to present accurate, up to date, and reliable, complete information. No warranties of any kind are declared or implied. Readers acknowledge that the author is not engaging in the rendering of legal, financial, medical or professional advice. The content within this book has been derived from various sources. Please consult a licensed professional before attempting any techniques outlined in this book.

By reading this document, the reader agrees that under no circumstances is the author responsible for any losses, direct or indirect, which are incurred as a result of the use of information contained within this document, including, but not limited to, — errors, omissions, or inaccuracies.

Contents

Chapter 1:
Eliminate Social Anxiety in Less Than 60 Seconds _____ 1

Chapter 2:
Make A Kickass First Impression _____ 13

Chapter 3:
Start A Conversation with Anyone _____ 31

Chapter 4:
Building Massive Confidence _____ 46

Chapter 5:
Charisma on Demand _____ 67

Chapter 6:
Instantly Persuade People _____ 76

Chapter 7:
Get Respect Immediately _____ 86

Chapter 8:
How to Analyze People _____ 96

Chapter 9:
How to Think Under Pressure and Crush It _____ 107

Chapter 10:
How to Sell Anything to Anyone All the Time _____ 113

Chapter 11:
Use Psychology to Get What You Want _____ 127

Chapter 1:
Eliminate Social Anxiety in Less Than 60 Seconds

Lots of individuals recognize social anxiety disorder as social phobia. One of the core features that define it is the fear of rejection in performance or a social scenario, being evaluated negatively, or being judged.

Individuals who are dealing with a social anxiety disorder may worry about seeming noticeably anxious or being categorized as boring, silly, or strange. Due to this concern, these individuals often stay away from performance or social situations. However, when they are unable to avoid a situation, they deal with intense distress and nervousness.

Lots of individuals suffering from social anxiety disorder also deal with physical symptoms. These could range from sweating and nausea to an elevated heart rate. They may also deal with these symptoms when dealing with a situation they fear.

Although these individuals understand that the fear, they are experiencing is not reasonable, they usually feel helpless against their anxiety.

Social anxiety disorder tends first to present itself in adolescence. Even though people diagnosed with this condition frequently report that they dealt with excessive shyness during their childhood, it is crucial to understand that this disorder is not just intense childhood shyness that has not been appropriately treated.

Mastering Your Mind

To overcome social anxiety and shyness, the first thing you need to do is to become the master of your mind. There are various ways to become the master of your mind. Here are some easy steps to take:

Listen to What Your Mind Has to Say

Listening is the first step to becoming the boss in any scenario. To be a good boss to your employees, you must listen to them. The same also applies when establishing yourself as the master of your mind.

As you listen, you also begin to acknowledge the things that the mind has been doing for you. Show a sign of gratitude for all its efforts in the past.

Come to Terms with Your Mind

The same way you cannot build a business without the help of others; you cannot survive without your mind. As a result, you need to accept the fact that you both need one another and are going to be together for life.

This step will allow you to accept the negative thoughts that you experience, so you do not waste willpower and energy trying to deny it.

Take Time to Study Your Mind

Using the art of mindfulness, you will be able to follow your mind as it moves from one thought to the other and learn how to focus the mind on a task.

What Can Social Anxiety Disorder Cause?

Social anxiety disorder can result in damage to the lives of those experiencing it. For instance, a person may not accept an enticing job opening that would require him/her to interact with new people frequently. It may also result in individuals staying home, as opposed to heading out with friends, due to worry that while drinking or eating, they would be unable to stop their hands from shaking.

Symptoms can be so drastic that they could hamper an individual's daily life and can cause significant interference with social life, performance at work, or their daily routine. This would make it difficult to complete an interview, participate in school, or get a well-paying job. In some cases, it equally prevents people from having romantic relationships and friendships.

Individuals who are dealing with this condition also have more danger of attaining serious alcohol abuse and depressive disorders. Even with the range of effective treatments available, a minimal number of individuals with this condition seek treatment yearly.

Triggers of Social Anxiety Disorder

Social Anxiety Disorder is a psychological condition that can be triggered by various situations. It could be triggered when attention is centered on you, when you are to give a speech, or when people make fun of you. Basically, you are not entirely comfortable with making new friends.

People who suffer from social anxiety experience different kinds of triggers. When this happens, they prefer to be anywhere but in that place. "Illness of lost opportunities" - this is how psychologists define social anxiety disorder. This is because opportunities may present themselves in situations that you find strenuous, and as a result, these opportunities are never explored.

What Are the Symptoms of Social Anxiety Disorder?

Social anxiety can be experienced in various stages. Different individuals experience these stages differently. For some people, it is experienced right before social scenarios, and it could be the fear of meeting people, the fear of speaking, or the anxiousness of being in the same room with strangers.

Sometimes this anxiety presents itself during the event, where the person suffering from social anxiety is experiencing nervousness, an anxiety-attack, or discomfort. They desire to be anywhere but where they find themselves. For others, it is after the event. They generally worry retroactively about their performance and how people saw them, what happened, and how they messed up. They try to avoid reliving similar scenes, and as such, stay indoors or avoid experiencing situations they consider nerve-racking.

The first step to take is to narrow down your social anxiety behavioral pattern. You must be able to identify what is peculiar to you and what ticks you off so you can eliminate it. There are ways an individual who suffers from social anxiety have learned to cope with it. For some, they become rigid in their movement. For others, they indulge in bad habits like drugs or excessive alcohol use to stop feeling the way they do. Others make sure no one ever sees them in the front row, and they hide from the crowd. These adapted behaviors mostly do more harm than good. It offers a mirage of a solution that does not address the core problem.

The secret is to stop the pattern and try something different. At first, it might not be comfortable, but it is helpful. You will feel more in control when you use positive solutions to address your anxiety. The disadvantage of adapted behaviors is the control they have over you - and the belief that without them, you cannot overcome your anxiety. These behaviors are more negative than positive.

Getting Over Shyness and Social Anxiety

People with social anxiety seldom have a social life. The development of irrational anxiety over a social interaction is known as social anxiety. It is a mental health condition that often leads to a lonely environment for such individuals. They often worry, and are very nervous about, how people see them; therefore, they have a strong desire to stay by themselves away from any social gatherings.

Some of the effects are depression and lack of self-esteem. To deal with this condition, they resort to excessive alcohol consumption and are often under the influence of drugs.

People dealing with social anxiety are mostly seen as irrational. A person with a healthy mental mind cannot understand why it is difficult to interact with another person, so they often give advice such as, "You've got to let go," or, "You need to face your demons." Social anxiety patients might be quite aware of the irrationality in their behavior, but this doesn't help since they cannot do anything about it on their own.

Curing social anxiety is not something that is done overnight. It takes time, but with diligence, it can be contained, reduced, or overcome.

There are people around us who live with this condition, and it could even be our family members or friends. If their situation is chronic, it is advisable to visit a physiologist or a therapist. A great benefit of this eBook is the inclusion of different methods one can try out to approach social anxiety:

Engage in Self-Love and Show Kindness to Yourself

The first step to consider when dealing with social anxiety is to have regard for your well-being and happiness. Put yourself first, and you must start mentally. There are times when you hear an inner voice that is always negative. It tells you how you are not good enough and how you do not deserve happiness.

You must understand that the power to change this narrative is in your hands. How do you do this? You talk back to that voice because all you hear are your fears and not the truth of your person.

So, here's a secret, when the negative inner voice talks to you, respond to it with exactly what it told you, but in a positive narrative. If your negative thoughts are about failures, respond with a situation when your failure gave you an insight into solving a problem.

You should also exercise self-love thrice a day, hug yourself, look at the mirror, and smile.

It sounds crazy, but it works! You must see through the negative voice that desires to diminish your uniqueness and embrace who you truly are.

There are times when you will be very nervous and shaky; it is normal, so do not quit on yourself. Take a deep breath, acknowledge the feeling, admit it, and move forward. It could be something else, but whatever you feel, realize this feeling. If you can accept it, it holds no power over you.

The Power of Positive Planning

Most times, social anxiety starts before the social gathering itself. How? The person is thinking and trying so hard to figure out how to fit in with the crowd, how to react to people, and how to respond during conversations. Just imagine the headache from having to figure all of that out even before the event.

The one true way to overcome, manage, or reduce social anxiety is by being an optimist and planning positively. If you are to plan the future social interactions with others at the event, think and act positively. If you must plan on what to say, believe that it will turn out well.

Sometimes, it makes it easier if you can own up to your feelings during a conversation. Simply telling the other person that you are a very shy person is another way of embracing your true self.

Your Small Successes Call for A Celebration

It is very easy to forget that you have made progress, such as when you successfully stay until the close of an event without running home or throwing up (yeah, it could be that serious). To make progress, it is important you take note of your little wins.

So, you should always celebrate whatever worked for you at a social gathering. It could be your ability to not spill a drink or that you were able to hold a conversation for 5 minutes or less. Whatever it may be, make sure you take note of them and celebrate them. Sensing you are making progress encourages you to want to try more.

Become Inquisitive

The genesis of social anxiety starts with this thought, "What will they think of me?" It then makes everything about you. How you interact with people, how well you perform in public and every other experience that follows.

The second step is to remove the focus from you! It shouldn't always be about you. It should be about the next person. Be curious about them. What are their areas of interest? What do they do? Do they like singing or watching movies?

When you successfully focus on the other person, you will enjoy having conversations with others. You can just listen to what they have to say, and you don't have to do the talking.

Step by step you will begin to enjoy the company of other people without the anxiety of trying to function in a socially acceptable way. Do not compare yourself to others. At the same time, do not judge others, as this will only make you anxious. Enjoy the uniqueness in our personalities and be entertained by it.

Build Confidence

Confidence has been said to mean, "the belief that anything is possible by taking action and by believing in oneself." Having confidence does not come easily to a person with social anxiety; therefore, it must be grown through practice.

You can build your confidence using various methods; it could be the way you dress, walk, or talk. If you are unsure of how to start, look out for people you admire and consider to be confident, then try to model after them.

Walk tall, talk naturally, and dress well. This will give you the needed boost to stand and interact with others. As I mentioned earlier, never compare yourself with another person, as you will lose confidence in yourself. Simply identifying areas where you know you have shortcomings and then following the steps of someone you admire can help.

So firstly, be natural, practice how to look confident in front of your mirror until you have a hang of it. As it is popularly said, fake it until you make it.

Simplest Tips to Eliminate Shyness In 60 Seconds

The tips below are applicable anytime you start to feel anxious or during a social situation.

Overcoming the Voice in Your Head

One of the reasons why a shy person will often have difficulties communicating in public is due to a shy voice in their head. If you are shy and you want to master your mind, then you need to overcome this shy voice. There are a few steps you can take which are discussed below:

Letting the Voice Know That You Are Up to The Task

One of the things that the shy voice in your head tries to do is to make you think you are not up to the task. If you fall for this trick, you begin to accept that you are not good enough. It may also bring up comparisons between you and close friends or family members.

If you keep waiting for external interference to tell you that you are capable of so much more, you may end up a failure. It is important you let the voice in your head know that you believe in your skills.

Overcome the Voice Through Failure and Growth

The only way to experience growth as a human is through failure. When you fail, you get feedback. The feedback helps you to understand the areas where you went wrong so you can make changes. By letting the shy voice realize that failure is part of the process, it becomes difficult to stop you from taking actions.

You will also gain more insight into the best ways to tackle future challenges.

The Importance of Saying Thank You

Appreciating someone is the best way to minimize their negativity towards you. The same also applies to the voice in your head. Since it is talking to you with negativity, saying thank you is a positive response to show you are not trying to fight the voice.

Identifying the positive intent of the voice is the first step. The voice may be telling you to avoid riding a bicycle because of the injury you sustained the last time. You can reply by saying "thank you for trying to keep me safe, but I have overcome my fear."

To apply this tip, create a list of the

As the voice slowly fades away, you will get the opportunity to take charge.

Show That You Can Step Out of Your Comfort Zone

The only way the voice in your head will win this battle is if you decide to stay in your comfort zone. Your ability to accept uncertainty and discomfort is one of the best ways to quiet the voice in your head.

It may merely be trying to prevent you from embarrassing yourself, but this will limit your chances of evolving.

Give Clear Details of Your Achievements

Why does this voice want you to believe you are not good enough?

It is merely because it believes that you have not made any positive progress. In truth, there are plenty of cases where you have been faced with adversity and come out on top. Let the voice know about all these cases.

Give Yourself A Period During Which You Don't Get to Do Anything

The main problem with social anxiety and shyness are the various thoughts running through your head. Your body will also be tempted to do something, anything at that moment, other than remain in the current situation.

To eliminate social anxiety quickly, the first step is to give yourself a brief period where you don't do anything either during a conversation or presentation. It is you falling into a worst-case scenario. It can be your worst-case scenario since it can be embarrassing when it seems like you don't have anything to say.

Once you can experience the worst-case scenario, you can eliminate the fear of failure.

When you are not doing anything, you don't talk or move. Just exist in a free form.

Preparation

Preparing beforehand can provide the boost you need to overcome any situation you find yourself in. It is an essential tool you have at your disposal as a person with social anxiety disorder.

The first thing you want to do is to commit yourself to the situation. Understand that you are unable to change what will happen. Accepting a situation will also help promote authenticity. You should also remind yourself of the reason for the interaction.

Other excellent ways to prepare yourself for whatever is going to happen is to read and write. Reading provides the inspiration you need while writing is a simple skill that can help unlock the real you. You can read on different topics such as history, cooking, or geography. As a result, you can improve your knowledge and vocabulary.

There are various things you may decide to write, and it may include different questions you expect to answer.

You should also find a way to calm the mind either by meditating or listening to music. You can also improve your energy levels by deciding to treat yourself when it is all over.

Chapter 2:
Make A Kickass First Impression

It is called a first impression because you only have one chance to get it right. It also takes just a few seconds to fully assess a person you are meeting for the first time.

A first impression covers both the verbal and nonverbal aspects of an individual. By assessing these two aspects, an individual can decide if they like you or not.

Nonverbal Cues

Smile

Positivity is something you want people to link with your brand as well as yourself. There are various expressions that you can associate with positivity. The most common manifestation is a smile.

There are lots of features that are easy to notice when meeting a person for the first time. One of the features that leave a lasting impression is a great smile.

Smiling has excellent benefits. It has a positive influence on your health, as it minimizes stress hormones. It also creates more comfort when you are around others.

Just because you need to smile doesn't mean you should force it. You may be trying to hide your nervousness with a broad smile. A grin is also very inauthentic. A grin usually has one side of the mouth open to reveal the teeth at one corner. It can often be interpreted as a sign of arrogance.

A genuine smile which is also known as the "Duchenne" smile is appropriate. The Duchenne smile activates the zygomatic major muscle and the orbicularis oculi muscle that expand the cheek and form wrinkles around the eyes respectively.

A fake smile only activates the zygomatic major muscle since it is the only one that we can control voluntarily. It is the reason why it is possible to tell a fake smile by covering the mouth of an individual. There is no sign of the smile beyond the mouth area.

Your Handshake

When meeting someone for the first time, a handshake is a significant gesture. Through a handshake, you can exude confidence and appear to be a polite individual.

Getting the handshake right is also very important. Your handshake can create a lasting first impression on anyone you meet.

To give a proper handshake, there are things you should do and others you need to avoid.

The first thing you want to do is to ensure that your hand is in a straight position all through the process. Another good tip is to make direct eye contact with the other individual. This usually implies that you want to establish a connection.

The next and most crucial part of the handshake is the grip. Your grip should not be too firm, and it shouldn't be weak. It is also vital that you don't shake with sweaty palms. This will disgust the other individual. Two easy ways to deal with sweaty palms is to make use of antiperspirant lotion and to have an alcohol-based hand wipe within reach.

The last step is to determine how long the handshake should last. This is often very difficult to determine. In an ideal situation, a handshake should have three pumps. If you are in a rush, then a single pump will do.

There are certain aspects of the handshake that can be difficult to perfect on your own, such as the grip. For more positive progress, call some of your brutally honest friends to help you out. Give them a handshake and let them compare it to others they have experienced over the years.

Body Language

Body language is a critical aspect of a first impression. Depending on how you use your body language, you can make a memorable first impression.

When interacting with someone, we often copy the body language of the other person. It is the same way in which you instinctively smile when your friend starts to smile.

If you can mirror the body language of someone you are meeting for the first time, you will make them feel like you both share some similar qualities.

The nonverbal cues that you observe during the conversation are the things your body automatically picks to display. Since it will also prompt the same emotions, there will be a form of trust that you will develop.

Make the Most of The First Ten Seconds

How you use the first ten seconds of meeting a new person is very important. Your introduction should be your focus in these ten seconds.

There are different phrases you can use when introducing yourself to someone new.

If you are introducing yourself professionally, you can say "My name is John, and I'm a freelance writer. I create high-quality content that clients can post on their blogs and websites."

It is always essential that you ask the name of the other individual if you are going first.

Some things that help when introducing yourself include the following:

- Preparing short answers for basic questions about yourself

- Focus on the things you share

- Understand the context. Is it social or professional?

- Avoid saying too much

A verbal introduction is a very productive process you can also use in remembering names with ease. You can start by repeating the name immediately and make a comment on it if possible. You can also repeat the name during your introduction.

A mental association of the name with an event also helps.

It Is Rude to Have Your Focus Elsewhere

Distractions are quite common in our daily life. Technology in the form of our computers and smartphones make it very easy to fall for your distractions.

If you are meeting with someone for the first time, the biggest mistake you can make is to shift your focus to something else.

A great first impression is all about establishing a meaningful connection. There is no way to develop this connection if your attention is on your smartphone or the YouTube video playing on your computer screen. You can't use the pause button on things happening around you.

People will want to be around you more if they are sure that you usually pay attention to them. Attention is not easy to get from everyone. Therefore, people will always remember anyone that offers it with ease.

Be Confident When You Speak

When making a first impression, you want to be noticed. If you are unable to convey your message, it becomes easy to achieve the opposite effect.

It doesn't matter the number of ideas you have or the great advice you can give; no one will listen if you are not confident. Be calm when speaking. This is an excellent tip to make you sound more confident.

You don't show confidence by being the loudest in the room. Don't become a nuisance to others.

Don't Avoid Eye Contact

Interest and confidence are essential traits you need in developing a great first impression. Having direct eye contact with the person you are meeting can help express these traits.

Everything must be done with a touch of professionalism. People will assume you are just staring if you don't take your eyes off a bit. There should be short intervals when making direct eye contact, during which you shift your gaze to the side. Avoid looking downwards so you don't appear timid.

If it seems like you are spending more time looking in another direction, it is easy to assume that there is something else more important than the conversation. Making direct eye contact is a sign of respect in some countries, such as the United States.

Verbal Cues

Listen More and Ask A Few Questions

Listening to people when they speak is an excellent way to make a great first impression. When you listen, you are showing that you care about others. If you try to be the one talking for most of the conversation, it is a clear sign that you like to be the focus of every conversation.

In a conversation, the best time to speak is when you are asked a question, or you have something of importance that will be beneficial to the other person. If a topic or advice applies to you, it may not have an impact on the other person.

While listening during a conversation is necessary, it is vital you don't seem like a boring person. No one enjoys a one-sided conversation. While listening, you should also ask some significant questions. These questions should relate closely to the topic of the discussion.

Asking questions is a sign that you have an interest in the other individual. It is also a sign that you are not just nodding your head, but also gaining insight into the topic.

Give A Compliment on The Little Things

Getting a compliment is one of the things that makes everyone feel good. A compliment may be based on something as simple as punctuality. It is a great feeling to know that someone appreciates the effort you put into arriving on time.

Although a compliment may seem quite simple, it is impossible to get enough compliments.

To start a conversation, complimenting people on minor details can go a long way. In addition to improving their mood, it is also proof that your attention is on them.

A good compliment is also an easy way to reinforce positive behavior in an individual you are interacting with. For example, you can say thank you to a person for their punctuality.

Let Others Know How Important They Are

The main point of a conversation is often to learn new information. It can be personal information or a different perspective on a topic.

It is critical you understand that you won't be able to learn anything new if you are the only one talking during the conversation. Your perspective and opinions will not change if you don't give yourself the opportunity to listen to others.

There are a lot of people that know things that you don't. The only way to acquire knowledge is by learning new things. Anyone you are conversing with will have a unique lesson for you, and this makes them very important to you.

Don't Expect Anything in Return for Giving

When trying to make a good first impression, go in without any expectations. Meaning, you should not expect anyone to offer anything in return for whatever you have to offer.

You may be offering free tips, excellent advice, or work-related assistance. The only way to make a great first impression is to do all these without thinking of what the other person can do for you in return. You will come off as being self-centered if your focus is only on what you can gain.

If you want to form relationships and create a real connection with others, you should only focus on giving to others.

Carefully Select the Words You Use in A Conversation

Consider these two phrases; "I get to go to the movies with Lisa tonight," and, "I have to go to the movies with Lisa tonight."

Both phrases convey the same message but in entirely different manners. In both sentences, the message is merely going to the movies with Lisa tonight. The use of "get" and "have" quickly changes the impact of each message.

In the first statement, there is a feeling of joy that the word "get" elicits. On the other hand, the word "has" defines the outing as a compulsion.

This is how your use of words can affect the feelings of others towards you. The words you use in your sentences should make people feel good about themselves.

Is Gossip Necessary?

Gossip can be challenging to understand. As much as everyone likes to listen in on a bit of gossip, do you think there is love for those spreading the gossip?

Good gossip is often a negative view of another individual. It gives an opportunity to share a good laugh at the expense of others.

How do you think people feel about others that share gossip?

If you share gossip with people, they are going to wonder if you do the same about them. Will he also laugh at me in my absence?

Gossip often makes people lose their respect for you as an individual. Imagine the impact it would have when trying to build a good first impression.

How Do You Deal with Your Shortcomings?

Humility will carry you a long distance when creating a lasting first impression. It takes humility to admit when you make a mistake. Be open to sharing cases where you have made huge blunders with others. It makes you more relatable with whoever you are conversing with.

Let people use your experience as a guide to avoid making the same mistake. If you are willing to laugh at your mistake, others will be inclined to laugh with you. This is a lot different from going behind your back to laughing at you.

If you have a good sense of humor when discussing your mistakes, people tend to gravitate towards you more.

Remember Their Name and Use It Often

You must have had a situation where you came across someone you met earlier but can't seem to remember their name. This can make a massive dent on the impression they have of you.

If you are meeting someone for the first time, exchanging names is usually part of the opening ritual. As the conversation progresses, ensure you make use of the name often.

There are two benefits of using their name during the conversation. Firstly, it implies that you were listening while they were talking. Secondly, it shows you like the person enough to remember their name.

With the kind of link, we have with our names, hearing someone use it often naturally makes it easy to remember the person. You should also be careful about how you use the name. You don't want to sound condescend.

If you avoid using a person's name, it can sometimes imply that you do not acknowledge them as an equal.

Things That Ruin A First Impression

Invading Their Personal Space

In simpler terms, you can define this as close talking. No one wants to smell your breath. It doesn't matter how fresh it is now.

A suitable method of measuring the appropriate distance is to use an arm's length. At this distance, you can hear the other person clearly. You will appear to show a lack of interest if you are standing too far away while standing too close may be a sign of aggression.

Choosing the Wrong Topic for A Discussion

If you are meeting someone for the first time, there are many topics you need to avoid. Personal finance, religion, relationships, and politics are some of the topics you should avoid at all costs. These topics can bring out an emotion that will ruin a conversation.

When talking about politics or religion, there are usually two extremities. If you are passionate about one extreme and the person you are conversing with has a passion for the other extreme, then it may be difficult to create a positive impression.

Also, avoid gossip and health issues. No one wants to listen to you go on and on about your exercise routine or diet.

Some good topics of discussion include travel, arts, sports, and entertainment.

Poor Body Language

When do you think you begin making your first impression on someone? Is it as soon as you start speaking to them? Is it as soon as you walk into the room?

Your first impression starts the moment you walk into a room. Therefore, you need a good body language. Body language speaks volumes about the type of person you are.

Your walking posture is crucial. If you are walking with slumped shoulders and your head facing down, then you don't project confidence. You want to walk with great posture. Let people feel they can rely on you.

A great posture implies that you carry your body in the right way. It refers to how you sleep, sit, stand, and walk. Steps to take to improve your posture include maintaining a healthy weight and being active. There are other steps to take in improving your posture in specific areas.

People can be watching you at any time. always Form a habit of using an excellent walking posture. It is better to be on the safe side.

Attaching No Importance to Names

Saying you are terrible with names is not an acceptable excuse by any standard. You are just being plain rude. It can also signify a lack of interest.

The same also applies to using the wrong name. Ask anyone that has made the mistake of using the name of their ex to refer to someone they just met.

Paying attention to minor details is very important in a conversation.

Avoiding Eye Contact

If you unable to make eye contact during a first meeting with someone, you are creating a terrible first impression. There are different messages you can pass across when you avoid eye contact.

Some people may interpret it as you are lacking interest in the conversation. People may also think you are lying or hiding something when you avoid eye contact.

When trying to make a good first impression, maintaining eye contact will show confidence, interest, and intelligence.

Phrases That Make Your First Impression Forgetful

"It Is Great to Make Your Acquaintance. And, What Is Your Name Again?"

You arranged a meeting with someone, and you even wrote it down in your schedule planner. The day of the meeting arrives, you are there on time, but if you use the phrase above as your opening line, it is not ideal.

This is because it says a lot about you as a person, as the other party thinks you do not value people and did not place much significance on the meeting in the first place.

You can understandably be the nervous type of which is why you forget names during a first-time meeting. Try to memorize the name of the person hours before the meeting to avoid embarrassment.

"I Can…", "I Am…", and More Self-Absorbed Phrases

Continuously using 'I' in a conversation implies that you are a self-absorbed individual. No one will have an interest in a conversation where all you do is boast about your achievements. You are making the entire conversation about you.

To make a killer first impression, don't become the focus of the conversation. If you have the opportunity, be the one to ask a question about the other person. Steer the conversation in such a manner that in the end, you will have learned a lot about the other person and have also said a lot about yourself.

"How Much Is Your Pay?" And Other Phrases Relating to Income

This is a particularly rude question to ask of someone you have just met. It is also an unwelcome intrusion into the personal space of that person. You do not have reason to ask such a question as it is none of your business at the time.

"Congratulations! Is It A Boy or A Girl?"

There is nothing worse than assuming that a lady is pregnant and then being wrong. It is a line you must never cross. Before you congratulate any woman on her pregnancy, be sure to get your facts right.

It is best you avoid this topic entirely when meeting someone for the first time. If you make this mistake, you may never get a chance to apologize.

"It Cannot Be Done," Or, "It Is Impossible"

Why would you want to portray yourself as a person with a negative attitude? That is precisely what you are saying to the other person, even if you do not say it outright. No one wants to be around people with negative energy, so saying this at the first meeting with someone is not a great idea. It shows you are not looking to see positives in situations that seem dire, which is a big turn off. People do business with people who give off positive vibes.

"Mum"

This word is mainly a filler in a conversation that tells the other person you lack confidence. It also makes the person you are conversing with easily lose focus on what you are saying. It is easy to distract people when you use "Mum" at the start of your sentences. In situations where you cannot answer a question on the spot, take a few seconds to think before giving your answer.

"Your Appearance Is Not What I Expected"

Wow! So, are you saying you are disappointed? Are you trying to say my body is not appealing?

Well, this is a phrase that can be interpreted in a lot of negative ways. Don't make the mistake of using it. You may be uncomfortable with their dressing, but who are you to judge?

In most cases, the conversation may go on smoothly, but your snide remark will not go unpunished.

"I Did Not Like Working with My Previous Boss."

You do not start a conversation with someone you are just meeting for the first time by having a rant about your former employer; it is a big turn off. The person you are sharing this with could be affiliated with your previous employers in some way or may think you could also complain about him to others.

From another perspective, it may also give an impression that working with you will be difficult.

If it happens to be a job interview, you can be sure you are not going to be considered for the vacant position.

Conversations such as this should only be held with people who are very close to you.

"Are You A Believer?"

There are specific topics you should not bring up during the first meeting with someone or even in certain situations, like your workplace. Religion is a topic you would not want to start with, as many people nowadays find it too sensitive to discuss, or feel it is a personal matter. A conversation of this kind can take place after you have known the person for some time, but not in the initial meeting.

Using Pet Names

Calling someone you are just meeting for the first time by a pet name is wholly unprofessional. If you are in the habit of doing such, you might want to limit the use of such words. Some people find it irritating.

Imagine you go for a formal meeting and address the people you are meeting with by pet names. You are making a terrible first impression. Using a nickname also falls into this category.

To avoid falling into the pet name trap, address people the way they state their name during the introduction.

"Who Is Getting Your Vote in The Coming Election?"

Political views are somewhat like the case of religion. Everyone has a personal political ideology that they passionately stand for. Broaching this topic on your first day at a new workplace is not ideal, as you could be speaking with someone who is on the opposite side of what you believe.

This could have the effect of you being at loggerheads with the said individual, resulting in low cooperation and productivity in the workplace.

"Hope You Don't Mind That I Am Late."

This is an annoying line to say on a first meeting. Why would you hope your own time has not been wasted but would gladly waste the time of the person you are meeting with?

The person most likely created time out of a busy schedule to meet up with you and you have kept the person waiting for hours on end. In cases of unforeseen circumstances preventing you from being on time to the meeting, you need to give the person a call or send a message explaining the situation.

To make a better first impression, you could suggest to the person to pick a date and time for rescheduling the meeting.

"Let Me Be Honest."

This phrase is so damning as it causes people to think that you have not been honest or telling the truth from the onset. You do not have to say this phrase before you can get people to believe what you are saying. If you have something truthful to say, be blunt and say it outright.

"I Don't Like This Weather."

If you live in the tropics where rain is a regular occurrence or dusty and hot in the dry season, you should not start a conversation with complaints about the weather.

The person you are having a meeting with experiences it as well. This opening line lets the person see how unprepared you are and that you are most likely a complainer.

"I Do Not Like Monday Mornings."

We have all had a case of the blues on a Monday morning when we would rather sleep in than get up. You should then try to motivate yourself into a working attitude instead of making a lot of noise complaining about how you do not like Mondays. It is a turn off for people who do love the hustle and bustle of Monday mornings.

Why not find a permanent solution to your Monday blues instead of using it as an excuse for low productivity? For example, you could become a consultant in your field, thereby self-managing your workload, and working on days you feel most productive.

Chapter 3:
Start A Conversation with Anyone

Learning how to start and hold a conversation is an important social skill that you need to develop as an individual. It will come in handy if you are trying to build a relationship with someone new and when you are trying to interact with a prospective customer as an entrepreneur.

There are various tips to help you develop your ability to hold a conversation. Learning to implement these tips in a conversation will help you become an expert in the art.

Small Talk

One crucial skill that is very important in holding a conversation is small talk. People that learn to use small talk have an advantage when it comes to initiating a conversation and preventing awkward silences.

What Is Small Talk?

Small talk is a form of social communication that is informal and covers unimportant topics. It is a technique that assists in starting a conversation with an individual you are meeting for the first time. Mastering the art of small talk requires a bit of practice on your part.

Although there are lots of topics you can use in small talk, different topics apply to different individuals. To make small talk effective in creating relationships, you must determine the topics that work for you. Some small talk topics include career, sports, entertainment, and family.

What Are the Benefits of Small Talk?

Meeting new people is unavoidable in life. Forming a good relationship can also be quite tricky. To lay the foundation for building a great friendship, small talk can be your best option.

People with social anxiety can use small talk to make meeting new people easier, as specific topics tend to come up frequently. You can prepare for some of these topics ahead of time, thus entering an initial meeting with more confidence. There are other significant benefits of small talk which will be discussed below:

It Is Applicable in All Areas of Life

There is something about small talk that makes it very important. It is something that you can apply wherever you find yourself in life.

Do you want to close in on a major contract? Are you looking for a great place to start a new career? Are you having a gathering of friends? Do you want to interact with your colleagues at work?

In all the situations mentioned above, engaging in small talk is all it takes to make a person more comfortable around you.

You See Things from A Different Perspective

One of the significant benefits of small talk is the opportunity to gain a new perspective on specific topics. As a social communication technique, it is a great way to interact with people. Interaction with other individuals usually gives you a look at things from a different angle.

In some cases, you may also get smarter as you develop new ideas to solve a problem through these interactions.

Easy Source of Information

We often tend to leave our homes without having time to watch the news, especially if we are running late. Will your smartphone be able to give you all the information you need?

Although smartphones offer access to the internet, it is possible to miss relevant information if you don't type it into your search bar. Small talk gives the opportunity for people to share new knowledge with each other.

People with high intelligence often offer great information when they are engaged in small talk.

There Is Spontaneity in Discussions

A unique feature of small talk is the inability to determine where the interaction will end up. Sometimes, you may have the opportunity to learn about a new idea that can be beneficial to you. It may be information on a great job opening or an excellent investment opportunity.

If your discussions with other people only focus on work-related issues, you may never get the opportunity to learn about new things in life.

You Become More Likable

There is nothing more important than engaging with others. There are also lots of people that love engaging in small talk.

Engaging with people, in this case, doesn't mean you are requesting a file related to a job. The engagement, in this case, is often to find out about the well-being of others and to share information about some fundamental life issues.

People will appreciate you more if you take the time to talk about their favorite sport or ask about their family. It is also an easy way to earn respect.

Why Do You Need Small Talk?

In creating a relationship with someone new, or managing your relationship with your friends, small talk is crucial. It is a technique through which you can assess the things that help keep friends, colleagues, and family members in a positive mood.

During a conversation, there are different purposes of small talk. The way you use this technique can have a considerable impact on the outcome of any conversation. Here are some of the purposes of small talk when conversing with others:

It Helps to Initiate the Conversation

An excellent way to determine the best course to take during a conversation is through small talk. If you are meeting up with friends, small talk helps in assessing moods and determining the purpose of the meeting.

Small talk when meeting with someone new is how each person understands the intention of the other. It quickly becomes apparent if the conversation will have a positive outcome or if your interests do not align.

It Eliminates Awkward Silence During the Conversation

A lot of people find it very uncomfortable to have silence during a conversation. When having a serious conversation, there will be a time during which there will be no vital topic. Engaging in small talk can serve as a filler discussion until a more critical topic arises.

Thinking of a new topic in silence can sometimes be inconvenient to everyone in the conversation.

A Great Way to End A Conversation

How you end a conversation can often have a huge influence when creating a first impression. Bringing a conversation to an abrupt end can often imply that you do not want the relationship to grow further. It can also mean that you are not delighted with the outcome of the conversation.

Once you are done discussing essential issues, engaging in small talk is an excellent way to end the conversation. It is a great way to part on a positive note.

How to Engage in Small Talk

Learning about the benefits of small talk and why you need it doesn't make you an expert at making small talk. In truth, everyone will have a unique approach to making small talk. Nonetheless, there are specific steps you can take to improve your ability to create effective small talk.

Here are some essential tips you should apply to make excellent small talk:

Show Confidence

It is not easy to start a conversation with someone you are meeting for the first time. In most cases, anxiety usually destroys the opportunity for a great relationship.

If you decide to engage in small talk, then you need to be confident. Being confident in yourself and your abilities will eliminate the fear that comes with meeting a new person. You should start with confidence, end with confidence, and maintain your confidence throughout the conversation.

You can show confidence by giving a firm handshake, maintaining a good walking posture, and keeping your hands out of your pocket during a conversation.

Your Body Language Is Important

To put people at ease, your body language is essential. There are different ways your body language can influence small talk.

The first thing is to ensure you are giving appropriate distance. It means you should avoid close-talking. A lot of people don't like it.

Crossing your arms during a conversation may be very convenient, but it is inappropriate. You should also ensure your shoulders are facing the person, and you are maintaining direct eye contact. These show a sign of interest.

Don't Jump into Conversations

We often meet new people during a three-way conversation with someone you know. Both of you may have a mutual friend. If you find a friend of yours in a conversation with someone you don't know, be careful how you enter the conversation.

Assess the situation to determine if the conversation is open to other parties. You may need to subtly get into the conversation by looking for an opening. During specific conversations, a question may be thrown to anyone around. It may be a good time to make a positive first impression.

Pay Attention to The Environment

Preparation doesn't mean you have everything covered. It is merely a way to cover most of the crucial parts. During small talk, you may end up using up all your tricks reasonably quickly. At this moment, you need to use your surroundings effectively.

Taking note of minor details about the other person will be of help. For example, giving a compliment can be helpful. Things in the environment can also serve as excellent topics. You can start a conversation about seasonal changes if you notice leaves on the ground.

Use of Your Phone Is Not Allowed

Why should you try to talk to me if you are going to be on your phone throughout the conversation?

If you are conversing with anyone, you want their attention to be on you throughout the conversation. It is also what the other person expects. Using your phone during a conversation will show a lack of interest.

What Is Something Interesting About You?

Small talk is your primary tool to get to know others. There is no way you will get to know one another if there is no room for an introduction.

Since you are including your introduction in the small talk, your introduction should give an insight into who you are. It should also be something very fascinating.

Come Up with A Topic That Interests Both of You

A great way to connect with someone is to discuss a topic that you are both passionate about. Determining this topic may be quite tricky, but you can try to take hints throughout the conversation.

Finding a common topic is excellent, but it can also be a huge issue if you are not well informed. Just because you love a sport doesn't mean all your facts are right. You will be exposing yourself to ridicule if you keep giving wrong information.

Since identifying a common topic can be very difficult in some cases, then opting for a topic that you know is very interesting to most listeners is an alternative.

Listening Is Equally Important

Like a regular conversation, it is important you remember that small talk also involves two parties. It means that both parties need to talk as well as listen for the small talk to be successful.

Since you have a lot of information and new ideas to share, you should also be ready to let the other person talk. Listening is paramount. This is how you get to understand the perspective, experiences, and knowledge that is available from others.

How to Keep A Conversation Going?

Certain tricks can help prolong a conversation. These are also helpful to ensure that the conversation remains lively with lots of things to talk about. The longer the conversation, the more information you will be able to get when meeting someone for the first time. You can implement the tricks below:

Open-Ended Questions Are Important

A conversation where one person is asking a question and receiving one-word replies won't get very far. It is possible you are also giving room for these one-word replies.

To keep a conversation going for as long as possible, you need open-ended questions. Such questions prompt people to give a response that is longer and more informative.

If you want to keep a conversation going, you can ask a question such as, "What do you think about the premier league?" The response you will get from that question will be much longer than the response you would get if you asked, "Do you like premier league football?"

Learning how to use open-ended questions effectively will help to improve the quality and length of the conversation.

Open-ended questions may also be about personal life if you are not forceful. Also, avoid generic questions. For example, "are you fine?" and similar questions.

Use the Silence to Your Advantage

The same way silence during a conversation will make you uncomfortable; it also has the same effect on the other person. However, you can make the most of the silence.

If you have been doing most of the talking during a conversation, running out of topics to discuss may not be your fault. Anytime such a situation arises, then it is time to let the other person come up with a suitable topic for discussion. Most people will often come up with small talk as a filler until they can raise an original topic.

This is a sure tactic that works in most cases unless you are at a gathering where the person can leave to get drinks. Don't overthink everything.

Coming up with a great conversation topic may be quite easy for you. The main problem may be overanalyzing every possible outcome. As a result, you begin to hesitate.

Sometimes it may be a genuine fear that the topic may not be as attractive to the other person as it is to you. The same applies to opinions or facts you may have about an issue.

If you stop thinking, you can develop another technique which you can refer to as blurting. It is a technique that enables you to say whatever comes to your mind now. Once you can overcome the mental restriction you have set, you notice that you can hold a conversation for much longer.

Having a filter is still important, nonetheless. Not all words may be suitable for a conversation topic in a different situation.

Don't Stay in Your Comfort Zone

A lot of people have difficulties holding a conversation because they only do it when it is necessary. If you prefer to spend more time playing games than talking to others, you may become a better gamer, but you will have difficulties holding a conversation.

If you make it a habit to meet just one new person every week, it becomes easy to hold long conversations later. It is the same way you must practice your shots to become a better shooter on the basketball court.

Comfort is excellent, but it won't always provide the results you desire.

A Simple Phrase to Use

The more a person talks, the longer the conversation. There is an easy way to get a person to talk more. Simply use the phrase:

"That's interesting. Can I know more?"

There are various parts of this phrase that make it effective. It is polite, and it shows you have an interest in what they are saying. The fact that you have expressed interest will light a spark in them. Being polite is just the topping.

You should combine it with various other positive reactions to show that you are listening.

Use Special Events to Your Advantage

There are numerous special events you can discuss in a conversation. An upcoming football event like the World Cup or Champions League is excellent topic. It may be an upcoming event or one that has recently occurred. There are lots of benefits to using an event in a conversation.

The first is that most people know about these events. Opinions on these events will also vary depending on everyone. If you are in luck, you may even learn new facts and information on the event.

Talk About Something You Know A Lot About

This will be a topic you are passionate about. If you are passionate about a topic, you should have the upper hand regarding the volume of information you have to offer in a conversation. It's time to make the most of this knowledge.

The good thing is that you don't have to limit it to just one topic. You may be a game freak and a music enthusiast. It is also very fascinating to find someone who is knowledgeable in multiple areas.

Anytime a conversation gets quiet, you can try one of these topics as a filler. Don't appear to be aggressive about these topics and avoid forcing a conversation towards any of these topics.

Simplicity is also essential. Also, make it fun. Your fun gaming sessions may bore the next person.

Things That Kill A Conversation

As much as you want to keep a conversation going, it is essential you understand that there are certain lines you do not cross. Knowing the things that make a conversation come to a quick end and consciously avoiding them will help you develop into a better conversationalist.

Talking Too Much

As much as you want the other person to talk, you won't like it if the person is talking too much. People will get bored if you keep going on and on during a conversation. The occasional nod is just a way to make you think they are listening.

Everyone in a conversation should be an active participant. A conversation is supposed to be two-way communication. Don't be the type that decides to do the talking for both parties.

Sometimes, you may not be to blame for the situation. In a situation where the other person is not talking, you can easily switch to open-ended questions. If the person is a shy type, an open-ended question will always get them talking.

It is easy to notice the glint in a person's eye when they get the opportunity to let out ideas.

Not Trying

Now, I am putting you in the other position. What if you are not making enough contribution to the conversation? Putting in 10% while the other person must come up with 90% is not a good practice.

Try to achieve a balance where you are giving 50%, and the other person is also giving 50% in a conversation. If there is a question for you, avoid one-word replies. Elaborating on your responses can positively extend the conversation.

Making the Conversation Unsettling

You may meet someone who can hold a great conversation, but your actions may have a negative influence. Different actions can make a conversation unsettling.

If you have bad breath or halitosis, you may have to keep your distance. The distance will usually have to be a bit large, which can make hearing difficult.

If you are getting too close, it may also be a problem. Close-talking is not welcome. Just because you have fresh breath, doesn't mean anyone will be comfortable with close talking.

Talking too fast can make it seem like you are mumbling. You should be able to speak clearly so everyone can understand you. Speak at a moderate pace and avoid shouting or whispering.

Making direct eye contact is essential, but it is not the same as staring. If you continue to stare during a conversation, the other person will become uncomfortable. It may lead to a brief conversation.

Avoid motions that can be distracting. If you are tapping your feet, fiddling with loose change in your pocket, or rocking a chair, you are introducing distractions into the conversation.

Don't Be an Apathetic Conversationalist

Being apathetic means, you lack interest, concern, and enthusiasm. If you are apathetic, how do you expect anyone to converse with you?

There are different ways through which you can show signs of being apathetic. If you generally have your hands on your phone, or you keep scanning the entire room from time to time, then these may be clear signs.

There are various ways to avoid being apathetic. You need to make a conscious effort if you want to change. You can start by showing a sign of interest in the conversation. If you have any experience that is relevant to the discussion, share it, and ask questions.

You also need to avoid distractions during a conversation. Don't scan the room for anything more interesting than your current conversation.

It is also possible to be in a conversation with someone else that is an apathetic conversationalist. In this case, you can make brief pauses to get their attention anytime they shift their focus.

If your topic is interesting, then you won't have to worry about your partner losing focus.

Chapter 4:
Building Massive Confidence

Building confidence is critical if you want to relate to more people without being nervous. There are various reasons why it can be challenging to grow your self-confidence. Some people have difficulties with low self-esteem, while others suffer from personal trauma. If a child is judged using very high standards from a young age, they may grow up thinking they are not good enough.

There are some ways you can build your self-confidence. These take time and require consistency.

If you are ready, you can use the tips discussed below:

Desist from Thinking About What People Feel or Think About You

The moment you start thinking of what other people feel or think about you, there is a possibility of getting discouraged. You then refuse to do anything so as not to be judged. You prefer to remain idle over to avoid the risk of being criticized.

Worrying yourself about what certain individuals think or feel about you will continue to weigh you down and may hinder you from achieving your desired goals.

It is possible you have set goals for your future, which is a necessity. If you're an ardent reader of Tiny Buddha, it makes you understand that at a stage, you do away with people's thought about you. If you don't, the self-doubt will become a part of your routine.

Don't Compare Your Achievements to Your Friends or Colleagues

If you start using your present situation as a comparison to others, you will begin to have doubts about yourself. Also, comparing your achievements to your mates will always have an impact on your mood. You may also fail to realize that the achievements of your mates are not an accurate yardstick in measuring your personal progress.

There is one thing that you need to be conscious of, especially when you find yourself in this kind of situation. Understand that everyone will have a different pace when it comes to progress.

You will discover that you are able to make significant progress in your career and daily activities as soon as you decide to do things at your own pace. It becomes possible to pick tasks that you are passionate about rather than those that you see your friends engaging in.

What Makes You Doubt Yourself?

All you must do is to invest more time in performing in-depth thinking to determine the source of your doubts. The source of your self-doubt may be an activity that you find to be positive. Taking the perfectionist route may seem like a positive step to you but may also be promoting self-doubt. Avoiding these sources can eliminate the chances of health issues.

Locating the source of your self-doubt will provide a way to eradicate it from the mind.

Healthy Sleep

Due to the present-day lifestyle, having healthy sleep is another activity that individuals find difficult to achieve.

Individuals in the modern world rarely sleep. The amount of rest they get is also too little to provide the confidence boost they need when they are awake.

Your inability to get enough sleep can result in frustration due to impatience, anger, sadness, and depression. You may also become very sensitive to little things such as an employee that doesn't reply to your message quickly. These are closely linked to low self-esteem.

Adhering to a strict 7-8 hours of sleep per night is ideal for healthy sleep.

Sleep can be described as a situation in which the body refreshes and fixes itself, as well as creates hormones such as testosterone.

Some things you can do to improve your sleep include:

- Eradicating noises from external sources

- Sleeping early to wake up early

- Switching off lights when sleeping

Other advantages of healthy sleep include positive productivity and mental balance. Mental balance is a healthy state of mind that involves the elimination of negative tendencies and accepting the potential of the mind to be creative. It includes cognitive balance, attentional balance, emotional balance, and conative balance. Your productivity is your ability to create positive results using the various resources at your disposal.

How to Get Enough Sleep?

Getting enough sleep will undoubtedly increase levels of testosterone.

Go to sleep early or stay longer in bed to attain the maximum time needed for enough rest. At least for your general wellbeing, you need to ensure you spend the minimum seven hours required in bed.

Having adequate sleep is imperative. Make sure your phone is off, avoid consuming caffeine at night, and make sure you have a warm shower before going to bed.

Believe Your Instincts

Another method of overcoming self-doubt is to believe in one's voice and vision. People tend to believe you more if you believe in yourself and what you are saying. Express your thoughts as they come to you rather than in a manner which you think is expected of you. Expressing your own thoughts and ideas helps in developing your self-confidence.

Reduce and Cope with Your Stress

Stress disruptors include meditation, yoga, listening to your favorite music, or laughing with friends.

When you are under intense stress, the body will react by creating the stress hormone, cortisol. Increased cortisol levels mean testosterone will be difficult to establish. Therefore, it is imperative to make sure you properly reduce stress in order to maintain your levels of testosterone.

Don't take drugs that mess with your hormones. Make sure you don't take substances that are like estrogen in any part of your body, such as xenoestrogens, which can drastically reduce levels of testosterone.

To do away with these substances:

- Don't preserve food using any form of synthetic preservatives

- Avoid pesticides

- Consume vegetables, meats, and natural fruits

- Adopt the use of organic skincare products

Proper Nutrition

It is easy for people to focus on their body weight and shape rather than what they eat. Focusing on body weight can often result in low self-esteem. To avoid this outcome, it is more beneficial to focus on healthy eating habits.

Hormones, such as testosterone, require appropriate nutrients in order to be created. Therefore, you must make sure all required building blocks are provided.

Adequate consumption of minerals and vitamins, which are essential nutrients, is vital for the proper functioning of the body.

Undoubtedly, in recent times, it has been difficult to achieve a diet that is up to standard.

Predominantly for this purpose, it is advisable to have adequate and proper nutrition. If by chance it is not adequate, external nutrients like Vitamin D and fish oil can be used to supplement your diet.

What you should also consider when nutrition is involved, is the fact that excess sugar intake is hazardous to the body.

Some effects of high sugar consumption include a stop in the production of testosterone, increase in fat storage, as well as visual disruption due to damaged blood vessels in the body system.

As much as possible, make sure you reduce or stop consuming sugar.

Feeding Properly

Feeding properly is a significant prerequisite to sustaining a healthy body.

By feeding correctly, it means you have a proper combination of various classes of food that includes carbohydrates, protein, and fats. To build testosterone, there is a need to increase the intake of eggs, butter, yolks, coconut oil, and other saturated fats in your diet.

Sugar intake should be avoided so that levels of testosterone will not decrease. Also, other activities that are attributed to low levels of testosterone are drug abuse and excessive alcohol intake. Whether for fun or due to prescription medication, the use of drugs can have a detrimental effect on testosterone levels. It is therefore important you consult with your doctor if you have a prescription to get more information.

Identify Your Well-Wishers and Build Relationships

Nobody knows or has it all. It means that as humans, there is no one capable of doing everything by him/herself. A compliment is all we require sometimes, and your well-wishers are the set of individuals that compliment you regularly.

Therefore, there is a need to know your preferred well-wishers, relations, playmates, and age groups who have always stood by you.

It is now up to you to channel your effort into strengthening your connections with these individuals. They are around us; therefore, develop those connections and make sure you can gain the necessary trust.

Let Your Mantra Encourage You

There are lots of mantras that you may have created over the years that you often repeat in situations where you experience self-doubt. The slogans go a long way in informing you of your past, the challenges you have faced, your accomplishments, and your outlook on the future.

These sets of mantras make you realize the need to take things slowly, comfortably, and receive guidance from your instincts.

"You are loved" is a great mantra to use often. Self-doubt may come up when you are not feeling too good, and it can result in you concluding that you have been deserted. By reciting this mantra, you can keep on believing in yourself, and in the fact that there are people who love you for who you are.

It is possible that all of us will experience self-doubt at some stage, as it is a part of life. It is easy to observe as you progress in life, that self-doubt comes into play when you think the love you receive does not align with your expectations.

If you have the people who love you around, appreciate them, and follow through on your goals, you can eliminate self-doubt.

Spend time in positive assertions and trust mantras. Exchanging pessimistic thoughts with an optimistic mindset is a significant step that you can adapt to eradicate self-doubt. It may look a bit weird in the beginning, but through practice and repetition, you can use optimistic assertions to develop your self-confidence.

Encouragement from Others

There are certain situations where you also fail to identify your toughness; instead, you dwell more on your faults.

In such situations, try as much as possible to consult with others. Advisers have experience and have a broad view of people. On your own, you may not be able to find out the things they are able to help you with.

You can also get inspiration from their trust, which can spur you into believing in yourself.

Pay Attention to Work

Focusing and paying attention to the most important work in front of you will assist in managing your self-doubt. Having too much free time and your inability to focus on important tasks often give room for self-doubt.

Low Testosterone and How It Affects Confidence

In a study titled "Single Dose Testosterone Administration Impairs Cognitive Reflection in Men," the study shows that testosterone influences confidence in men. Low testosterone levels can also result in low energy levels, fatigue, and depression.

These are some of the common reasons why people lack confidence. To address these issues, it is important to find some of the causes of low testosterone and then identify the means of addressing these issues.

The increase in confidence from the reduction in cognitive reflection and an increase in the reliance on intuitive judgment.

Testosterone Killers That Mar Your Social Confidence

Processed Sugar and Carbohydrates

When we talk about processed carbohydrates, we do not only mean sugars. We are also discussing other foods that transform into sugars after ingestion. These foods include bread, rice, and pasta. Your system is programmed to react to sugars by producing and releasing a hormone called insulin. The rise in insulin levels in one's body is a disaster to produce testosterone in one's body.

Additionally, when we eat highly glycemic food, lots of processed carbohydrates can knock down one's testosterone level for a couple of hours. Over time, it could be worse if one makes the consumption of these foods a habit, as the body could become entirely insulin resistant. Aside from the fact that this is related to prediabetes, it's also related to very low-level testosterone production.

Carbohydrates with less sugar are still a healthy and essential part of a balanced diet so much so that carbohydrates produce required building-blocks for testosterone. However, staying away from processed variations of carbohydrates and sticking with nutritionally beneficial ones will neither increase your insulin nor lower your testosterone production. One important source of healthy carbohydrates is chickpeas. They also make a good source of proteins, fiber, and a considerable percentage of vitamins and minerals for testosterone production.

Stress and Anxiety Levels

It's possible you understand that stress and anxiety take tolls on your health. At the same time, you may not know that it also possesses some chronic effects on the levels of your testosterone.

Objectively, there exists an inverse relationship between cortisone, the stress hormone, and testosterone. Anytime cortisone rises, testosterone falls. Also, cortisone is not only linked with one's testosterone levels, but it has an impact on anxiety levels depending on the amount present in the body.

Do you sometimes seem not to feel alive because you had a difficult day? It might just be that cortisone has started to toll on your testosterone levels immediately. It's important to know that when prolonged stress is involved, it can be more disastrous, as the body stores up cortisone as it tries to contain your stressors.

Biologically, one's body enters 'flight mode', and reproductive strength isn't an immediate concern. The body prioritizes other functions, which makes one unable to manufacture testosterone at the highest level.

Getting to reduce stress in one's day-to-day activities or trying to work on ways to cope with it, is a primary objective towards increasing the production of testosterone in one's body.

Excessive Alcohol Consumption

You may have listened to, or personally seen, the worrying consequence that a night spent binge drinking has on your ability to do and be at your best. Nonetheless, are you in the know that alcohol consumption also affects many processes in the production of testosterone? The reality is that storing excess alcohol in your system can reduce your testosterone.

Concisely enough, whenever you have a drink or two, you may not feel the effect of it on your testosterone. When one's system breaks down alcohol, the process involved makes use of some coenzymes called NAD+, which is a vital part of testosterone production. If one's system lacks required building-blocks to produce testosterone, then it cannot produce more of it. This spot is where the impact directly correlates with the quantity of alcohol taken. Hence, taking unquantified drinks will not possibly have a reasonable effect. One must be aware that the more one drinks, the less testosterone is produced. On occasions of having a beer or other mixed drinks, it's unlikely to affect the testosterone levels, but when one frequents them, it's worthy to note that one's testosterone production will plunge.

Consuming Water That Contains Chemicals

Given that you're someone who's predominantly aware of your health standards, it's possible that you drink a lot of water to stay hydrated and keep your body running smoothly. Undoubtedly, water is a valuable commodity we cannot do without and it's vital for biological processes. Nonetheless, it's equally important that you see to the quality of the water you ingest because the inadvertent high intake of water is a passage for testosterone damaging chemicals.

You may think that moving to bottled water is next, but the reality is that companies are being regulated and are not given the freedom to release the rate of contaminants in their products.

Additionally, many damaging chemicals like phthalates or bisphenol-A (BPA) that are usually seen in plastic containers can get back into the water. It is advisable to try to filter water before drinking it and ensure you make use of safe containers.

Too Much Body Fats

Everyone knows that being overweight comes with some health risks. One of them for men is that it severely reduces their testosterone levels. Human body fats contain aromatase, an enzyme in the adrenal gland, which transforms androstenedione and estrogen.

What Is the Implication?

The only meaning to this is that the more body fat you possess, the more your testosterone gets turned into estrogen. Another issue is that testosterone is a hormone that is fat soluble. This means that it could be stored in fat tissues instead of floating freely in the blood, thereby reducing your testosterone levels.

Testosterone acts in a critical role in one's body synthesis. Hence, as one starts shredding the excessive weight while testosterone levels are high, it will aid in burning off the fat.

Dealing with Low Testosterone Exercises

Engaging in routine exercise is advantageous to your general well-being. Your testosterone levels can be increased with the aid of routine exercise.

Some forms of routine exercise that can help increase levels of testosterone are lifting weights, high-intensity interval training (HIIT), and resistance training. In adherence to the tenets of weightlifting, squats, deadlifts, and bench press should be included during weightlifting.

Expose Yourself to The Sun

Vitamin D that is derived from the sun has been described by researchers to have great benefits. It is also very useful in naturally boosting levels of testosterone.

Exposure to the sun is the best way to increase levels of Vitamin D. However, in some countries, exposure increases the risk of developing skin cancer. Most people get used to sun exposure and make use of sunscreens to shield themselves, which translates to little or no sun exposure. Failure to expose yourself to the sun can pose a risk for deficiency in Vitamin D3, which can be a reason for low levels of testosterone.

Nevertheless, Vitamin D3 supplements can work some magic, since there are few foods that contain this vitamin.

Use Natural Ways to Increase Testosterone

Natural supplements such as testosterone boosters are of immense assistance in increasing your testosterone levels without any problem.

There are several supplements that have been tested and proven to work effectively. Here are some of these supplements:

Zinc

Zinc is an essential mineral that is vital to many substances associated with the body system. As with Vitamin D, Zinc is essential in building and maintaining adequate levels of testosterone.

Consistently consuming a diet that is low in zinc may have an adverse effect on testosterone levels in the body. Foods that are rich in zinc include seeds, legumes, and beans.

Some other natural ways testosterone can be increased include:

- Ginger
- Ginseng
- Magnesium
- Fenugreek
- Selenium
- Horny Goat Weed
- Tribulus Terrestre's

Write Down A List of Things That You Show Gratitude for Daily

You don't have to subject yourself to mediocrity. There is no need to be cautious of what you possess and what you do not. Only thinking about what you have been unable to achieve will make you feel inferior and might have a negative impact.

Rather than channeling your energy on what you do not possess, be concerned about what you currently possess and what you have achieved. It brings an affection of gratitude, and when you channel your energy to gratitude, the changes you require will arise, and your future will be guaranteed.

An affection of gratitude brings an optimistic spirit from you. When you are optimistic, you're relaxed. Naturally, the joy in you will turn around to bring good tidings.

Read One Positive Book A Day
One of my adapted habits to quickly increase my level of believing in myself is to read my favorite books. You can pick a book from your favorite author to read daily.

Don't Seek Consent from Outside
In a situation whereby you allow other people's judgment to cloud your thinking, you automatically give others control over your life. Lack of control over your life often results in self-doubt. It's an endless chain.

Seek advice from people you believe will give you the right answers. Nonetheless, it is crucial you remember that you will always remain in control, regardless of the decisions you make. Although there might be consequences, you must not regret your decisions.

Getting Over the Inner Critic

A couple of books found on shelves explain methods to get over self-doubt. Many people make use of the terminology 'conquering doubt' in a manner that looks dismissive.

Everyone has doubts about being their natural self. The role it plays is to keep you safe, although, that safety lifeline can turn against you if you fail to be aware of its negative consequences.

Take some time to check the concept of doubt in your life. Have you ever wondered what resources you use to get yourself out of self-doubt when it comes up?

Every time we attain little victories, our confidence gets a boost, which weakens our self-doubt. Your inner critic is often like a speed bump in the form of self-doubt. The very essence of speed bumps is to make you slow down while driving, never to put you to a complete halt. Hence, a similar approach can be copied to phase through self-doubt.

Self-doubt may be causing massive havoc in you. Try to realign with your purpose instead of letting the challenges of self-doubt overwhelm you. Blaming past failures will only result in further destructive mindsets. Take firm actions on set goals and approach your doubts with compassion. You have the sole responsibility to realign them peacefully without any feelings of guilt.

Your sojourn to internal tranquility and achievement is filled with numerous challenges. Stick to them and face them with attention and zeal for success with the necessary hard work required.

Let Go of Your Negative Mindset

Verily, many people's minds are filled with a lot of garbage while growing up. No one was an exception. Depending on their personal struggles, some people undergo a form of priming that causes them to keep shut in most situations. This is the case with a stutterer.

By assuming that no one wants to get into a discussion with a person that stutters, these individuals try to avoid conversations. By avoiding conversations, there will be negative impacts in the form of lost opportunities.

Self-doubts come from the reverse thinking plaguing the lives of many individuals. Now, it's time to reset this mindset. You can use a combination of counseling, therapy, and recovery to help get over self-doubt.

Most times, people are not willing to engage in the tedious emotional work of accepting that they were hurt, either due to too much dependence or a fear of getting abandoned. These dangerous mindsets still lurk around you, and it might become increasingly difficult to attain freedom and the much-required self-confidence you need. When one has a broken arm, reading, eating, sleeping, or exercising will never fix it.

To achieve your dreams, the need to sharpen your mind becomes non-negotiable.

Getting Out of Your Comfort Zone

In order to achieve personal development, you need to be ready to try something different, even if you feel awkward and uncomfortable. Have you ever thought about your first-time swimming? You kept harboring the fear of drowning, so you didn't exceed the shallow end for safety purposes. But now, you may have even considered swimming in an ocean. This applies to life. Little steps taken out of your comfort zone will push you inch-by-inch to take fresh challenges. This is the beginning of your progress.

Failure Is No Big Deal

Researchers have shown that the most prevalent factor that makes self-doubt creep in is the fear of failure. Although you may be caught awestruck, many successful people of this century have discovered a failure to be indispensable on their road to success. Elon Musk, the great tech-entrepreneur, maintains that failure is necessary for innovation. By being practical and accepting failure at different points in one's career, one will be making tremendous progress in overcoming one's fears.

The More You Learn, The Better You Feel

Ignorance makes you anxious and scared, whereas knowledge makes you confident and self-assured. The more skills you acquire, the better your chances of being successful in life.

The reverse is also correct. Your chances of succeeding are significantly reduced each time you misuse your resources.

It is not necessary to learn every minute, but the best way to learn is to have adequate rest in between your learning periods. You tend to feel better with every bit of knowledge you acquire.

Do not allow fear to dominate your life. Ignorance can only bring you fear and anxiety, so learn as much as you can during your lifetime.

Own Your Accomplishments

You must take matters in your own hands if you want to experience a great turnaround in life. You do not have to wait for people to compliment you for your success. Instead, congratulate yourself first. Praise yourself every time you achieve something, no matter how little.

Make Self-Doubt Work for You

This may sound crazy, but it has been observed that a certain amount of self-doubt can enable you to stay sharp, inventive, and focused on the task ahead. Self-doubt can help you stay on track and motivate you to put more effort into achieving your goals. However, if it is not correctly managed, it might drag you down. Therefore, you must not let self-doubt bring you down, rather see it as a stepping stone to going higher in life.

Intermittent Fasting and Its Benefits

Intermittent fasting is a pattern of eating whereby you skip certain meal hours during the day. This does mean you are restricted to eating a kind of food or encouraged to avoid others, but instead, it determines when you should eat.

The methods of intermittent fasting vary, but they all center on splitting your meals for the day or week into fasting and eating periods. Fasting is nothing new to most individuals because you fast while you are asleep at night, which is the reason the first meal of the day is called breakfast. However, this fast can be extended beyond typical breakfast hours.

You can choose to have your first meal of the day at noon and have your last meal by 8 pm. This means you fast for 16 hours a day and have an 8-hour eating window for the day. The 16/8 method is one of the most popular methods of intermittent fasting.

Of all forms of fasting, intermittent fasting is the easiest. A lot of people can attest to this as they reportedly do not struggle through it, but rather feel good during the process. Hunger is only a challenge during the beginning process, but the body adapts quickly, and hunger is then no longer an issue. During the fasting period, only liquids such as water, tea, coffee and other beverages with few calories are allowed; this means no food during this period. Supplements with no calories in them are also allowed during intermittent fasting.

How Does Intermittent Fasting Affect Testosterone?

The intermittent fasting facts might be overwhelming, but they will undoubtedly convince you to consider fasting regularly if you desire to boost your testosterone levels naturally.

Testosterone Is Positively Correlated with Insulin Sensitivity

Skipping breakfast is a good way of increasing testosterone levels. This is because the moment an individual wake in the morning, the circadian cycle of the body has a natural cortisol spike. This falls in the period when a lot of people have their breakfast. With individuals who are considered healthy and already have high insulin sensitivity, certain food intake causes a spike in their insulin level. This means a high level of cortisol is circulating the body at that period of the day, which causes a drop-in blood glucose. As a result, a phenomenon known as "false hunger" is experienced, which causes an increase in the consumption of calories.

Skipping breakfast helps regulate cortisol, insulin, and blood glucose levels at the time of the day when they are easier to produce.

Production of Adiponectin

The hormone called adiponectin can also be increased through intermittent fasting. Insulin sensitivity of the body is increased as a result of an increase in adiponectin during fasting. A study has shown that adiponectin is powerful, as it can reverse insulin resistance in mice.

Excess Body Fat Can Be Burned During Intermittent Fasting

The body uses excess body fat as a form of energy for daily activities, and this allows the body to get rid of toxins early in the day before carrying out activities such as glycogen synthesis and digestion. Burning excess fat is one of the fastest ways to increase testosterone levels in the body. There is an inverse correlation between the fat level of the body and common measures of insulin resistance like HOMA-IR, C-peptide, and insulin. The adipose tissue is responsible for the inverse relationship between insulin resistance and testosterone but has nothing to do with the sex hormone binding globulin (SHBG).

This means that an individual with a high level of body fat will only produce a low level of testosterone naturally.

Boost in Growth Hormones

Growth hormone levels in the body can be boosted by about 2000% by fasting for just 24 hours. Growth hormone and testosterone levels work hand in hand at increasing training capacity, improving protein synthesis, and increasing the uptake of glycogen into the muscles.

Chapter 5:
Charisma on Demand

Charisma is your ability to influence anyone that is around you. If you are a charismatic individual, people will naturally admire you. Some people are naturally charismatic while others need to make a conscious effort to develop their charisma.

To build your charisma, follow the tips below:

Building Up Your Self-Esteem

There is a lot to be said about the importance of having a sense of high self-esteem or being confident in oneself. An individual who exudes self-confidence is optimistic about his personality and is at ease amid other people.

You can build your self-esteem by attaining set goals, such as becoming an expert in your field, being the individual that brings pride to the family, being a true friend, or being a law-abiding member of your society.

The definition of self-esteem could mean different things to you, as it is a matter of opinion, but let your principles be shown by how you react to specific actions. Once you have a sense of self-worth, people will be ready to give you that iota of respect just as you respect yourself. Interacting with people from different backgrounds becomes child's play when you build up your self-esteem.

Develop the Skills of An Interested and Exciting Conversationalist

One of the most important habits to develop as a person is the skill of being a great conversationalist. This means being an active listener to the person you have a conservation with and knowing when to chime in with your questions and your suggestions. Develop the charismatic attitude of asking questions to people about themselves rather than making the whole conservation about you. It eliminates the chances of people considering you to be boring and pompous.

A charismatic attitude equips you with the skills to make your fellow conversationalist feel good while conversing with you.

Social Awareness and Body Language

When during a social gathering, be quite observant and take note of certain things. Things like what the main topic of conversation is amongst the people that make up the interactive circle, the topics that are too sensitive to bring up, or the way you should portray yourself in such a gathering.

Try as much as possible not to have body posture that is read as being on the defensive in the minds of other people. Put out an open, receptive body posture, and you will find yourself being at ease wherever you are, even in the company of people you do not know. These individuals will also be more comfortable and find it easier to relate to you.

Positive Mental Outlook

Society does not relate well with individuals who are stiff, who cannot have a good laugh, and who tend to make a big deal out of any slight issue. Individuals with this type of temperament do not get invited to social gatherings as they are boring, and probably too controversial.

An individual who is known for his jovial, humorous, and positive outlook is seen as a necessary asset in social gatherings.

If you are of the melancholy type, try to be more light-hearted, be more humorous, and take life easy. This will attract people who will come flocking to your side in a social gathering. With this type of attitude, you will see yourself getting more invites to gatherings, meeting new people, and making new connections.

Emotional Facial Expressions

Psychologists have made it known over the years that showing more emotion through your facial expressions is a great way to be a person with charisma. Learning the art of being more expressive with your face shows how much you empathize with your fellow individual. You can practice how to facially express different emotions in the confines of your room, and by asking people how well you portray such emotional expressions.

Of course, there is a downside to being more facially expressive with emotions. People will find it easy to identify situations when you are flustered or in a rage. To counter this, you can also practice working on keeping facial expressions in check. It is not all the time you want people knowing what is going on with you.

Be an Active Listener

Another skill seen as a must towards developing a charismatic attitude is the art of being an active listener in conversations. Some books on psychology have come up with different definitions of what it means to be an active listener.

In a nutshell, it means listening with rapt and undivided attention to what the other party is saying instead of planning out your reply.

Knowledge of Body Language Signs

Having a basic understanding of the giveaway signs a person is showing through their body language is a skill you also need to work on. You can garner this knowledge by reading books on body language, attending seminars on the subject, or by being a keen observer of people and their different body postures.

It helps in knowing if a person is comfortable with your presence or not. You can also develop methods through which you can let people become more relaxed around you when you can understand their body language.

Sharing Personal Experiences with Stories

Research by many intellectual bodies has shown that individuals with charisma connect more with their listening audience by telling captivating tales of their personal experiences. Managers in big conglomerate firms have been put through some charismatic attitude seminars to teach them the art of using storytelling to motivate people under them to boost productivity.

Rhetorical Questioning

People do not like answering rhetorical questions. They usually feel it is annoying and a waste of time. However, it is a charismatic skill worth learning. You can use rhetorical questions to motivate individuals to be better people, or to focus on what is essential.

Set Personal Goals That Can Be Confidently Achieved

Studies have shown that a charismatic leader is an individual who sets defined goals for his team of individuals and believes they can achieve them. He instills belief and passion in each member of his team through this winning attitude. Team members would, as a result, work hard as a unit to achieve the set goals with lots of confidence.

Effective Use of Words in Communication

Individuals with charisma have been known to communicate effectively with the way they use words. They make use of words and phrases that make them connect on a personal level with the person they are having a conversation with. This can be quite soothing, especially in cases where an individual is very emotional.

Social Risk-Taking

As you build up confidence in your social interaction skills, you realize you can read social flows quickly. You become much more comfortable and positive in interacting with people on a social level with ease. You can further enhance your confidence by engaging in the act of testing yourself in uncharted waters by engaging in actions you would never have thought of doing socially.

What Really Is Social Confidence?

Self-confidence is, in simple terms, a personal examination of your abilities when it comes to engaging in an activity with utmost success. Think back to the first time you had to perform an activity like driving, skiing, or flying a plane. At first, you are going to be afraid because you know these activities can result in serious injuries or death. But with time, as you practiced these activates, you gained more confidence in your ability to handle these situations.

But it should be noted here that self-confidence and social confidence should not be misconstrued to mean the same thing.

While self-confidence is your trust in your abilities or skills generally, social confidence refers to your trust in your social skills and your ability to gain acceptance in a social setting. It is a targeted form of your confidence.

Being socially confident is a different thing entirely. The way you build your self-esteem is also applicable when you decide to improve your social confidence levels.

In a social gathering, you have many options available to you in terms of how you react, and what you say in any scenario. These options will seem daunting if you are not confident in your social interaction abilities, especially in matters of physical intimacy with the opposite sex or when you try too hard to fit in.

When you are socially confident, you tend to take more social risks. This is because as you face these social risks often in your daily social interactions, you become bolder and have no anxiety in taking such risks.

One must work on cultivating a charismatic attitude by working on personal social skill levels to a considerable extent. This makes for easily fitting in with any social function you find yourself.

Phrases That Kill Your Charisma

We just discussed some things you can do to become a more charismatic individual. These are tips you can incorporate in your daily life. Since those are things to add, did you think of the things you need to stop doing?

Pre-Emptive Disqualification

Most people make use of such phrases frequently. It is a method of setting the bar for the assessment of a speech or performance.

If you want to sing and then start a phrase with, "I am not very good but..." you are trying to tell people that they can judge your singing poorly. The truth is that you are putting a bias in the minds of your listeners. As a result of the bias you have set, it will be impossible to get an honest opinion from your listeners.

Saying "No Problem"

This is usually the easiest reply people come up with anytime someone says, "Thank you." This reply implies that you're helping them only because it doesn't have any impact on your life. It means that if it would have cost you something to make yourself available to help, you would not have been available.

There are various situations where this may become apparent. It may be a case where your friend asks for your help in moving to another apartment, or another in which your assistance is required in setting up a piece of new equipment.

You should make people understand that you are assisting them mainly because you value the friendship you share with them. Every time you get a thank you from your friend, it is an opportunity to develop your relationship further. Try not to waste this opportunity.

You can decide to change this phrase to another much more effective phrase like, "I am always happy to help." People will understand that you are trying to make your relationship with them much stronger. As a result, more people will be attracted to you as a person.

There are other situations where saying, "no problem," is not an issue. It may be a scenario where you help someone get a product from the top shelf in a grocery store. Here you are merely doing them a favor.

Saying, "You Messed Up."

Do you understand what it means to point accusing fingers? That is precisely what you are trying to do when you use this phrase. There are situations where you can use this phrase and get away with it, but in other cases, you are asking for a fight.

If you are in a grocery store and there is an error on your receipt, you may get away with telling the cashier, "You messed up my receipt." The only reason why the cashier will let it fly is that as the customer, you are always right.

When you say this same phrase to someone with whom you have a relationship, like your family members, friends, or partner, then you are asking for trouble. No one in this category is going to let you off easily.

A better option to avoid confrontation is to use a phrase that does not point an accusing finger. If there is something wrong and you want to correct it, you can use another phrase.

A phrase like, "There may be an error in the inventory. Could you assist me in fixing it?" is a better option.

In the first part of the phrase, you avoid blaming anyone. The error may have come from someone else entirely, so you don't want to blame the person delivering the records.

You can easily blame a person, and after rechecking, you find out there was no error to begin with. Using this phrase still gives room to accept that there is no mistake in the inventory records.

To avoid confrontation, the concluding part of the phrase forces the person you are discussing with to work with you. When you are both working towards the same goal, there will be no room for confrontation.

The second phrase minimizes resistance and makes the work go faster.

The Use of Negative Absolutes

Most situations where people use negative absolutes is during an argument. The use of a negative absolute can escalate the debate into a big fight. It is essential you take note of such instances in order to avoid them.

A phrase that depicts a negative absolute is the use of, "You never..." or, "You always..." before saying something negative. It is essential you avoid these statements as it can cause a considerable strain on a relationship.

Some typical examples of negative absolutes include the following:

- "You never have time for me."

- "You are always talking about your ex."

- "You never do the dishes."

- "You always think you are right."

Chapter 6:
Instantly Persuade People

Learning to persuade people is an important part of everyday life. There are times when you need things to happen in a way and getting people to do it is the only option.

Developing the right skills will help you persuade individuals and influence their decisions.

How to Persuade People

How Do You See This?

Remember that whoever asks the question whenever persuasion is involved is in control. This means the direction of any persuasive conversation lies in your hands if you are the one asking the questions. This is a great tool that helps you persuade the other person into agreeing with you.

This is essential, as it helps you connect with the other person, as it gives the impression that you understand them.

It is no secret that most people love to be heard and they enjoy doing the talking and sharing their opinion. Hence, you will have something to say when people ask us about themselves.

Therefore, asking this question allows you to understand other people's point of view concerning a certain point. As a result, a connection is built between you and them. You can utilize other people's opinions when passing across your point.

The moment you become able to see the things from the perspective of others; you will realize how you can use it to persuade others actively.

Accept Being A Data-Driven Individual

Although most people like to consider themselves as data-driven people, the majority are not. Whenever you ask a person whether they are data-driven, they most often say yes to this question.

The moment you get them to admit to being data-driven they are going to try to prove it to you. This is because they wouldn't want to be inconsistent or confused. There are six principles of influence that control decision making in humans and one of them is consistency.

This is an essential tool; the moment you get a person to agree to something, it becomes even easier for you to persuade them using the data you have.

Use Silence.

This is a powerful tool in persuasion.

When you keep quiet, you automatically force the other person into filling the silence. They may eventually slip up on something useful to you the more they talk.

Deliberately choose to not respond during a conversation when it's your turn to speak to find out what the other person would say. The chances that they would bring up something useful that would keep the conversation going is high.

This was a technique created by Esquire great Cal Fussman and later adopted by Tim Ferriss. Although it might seem counter-intuitive, it is an excellent way to establish a connection between you and other people.

One of the reasons why silence is an excellent tool in persuasion is that it is unexpected, and something that most humans like without even knowing it.

The next time you get into a serious conversation with someone, you can try it out. Give them the freedom to talk, nod and smile in agreement to whatever they are saying. This makes them believe you are following and would motivate them to keep talking. You will be amazed at how well this works in a persuasive situation.

Have You Thought Of...?

Always remember that humans are very emotional beings. We do not like to be doubted or disregarded. This is the reason a more subtle approach should be used when you want to question a personal judgment.

There is a possibility that the other person has thought about it but doesn't take it seriously when the question is asked; therefore, you can move on to making your thoughts known. If they haven't thought about it, you trigger them to consider it before voicing out their opinion.

Such a question is related to Pre-suasion. This means that if they haven't given prior thought to your question, the tendency that they would pay more attention to whatever you have to say is high. This puts you in control of the conversation, and you steer it in the direction you want, making it easier for you to convince the other person.

Sentences You Should Always Avoid

Now let's talk about the two phrases you should avoid during a conversation. We all find ourselves guilty of using them at one point or another. To avoid them, you must first be aware of them.

"Listen to Me!"

This is a statement that must be avoided in a conversation as it is in no way persuasive. Very often when we find ourselves in a heated discussion with friends or loved ones, we find ourselves making use of this sentence.

This hardly works because rather than appeal to the subconscious mind of the other person with a more convincing point, you come off as forceful because you have nothing new to offer, which is counterproductive.

"You Are Wrong!"

During an argument we most often find ourselves making use of this phrase just because we feel we are right, while the other person is wrong. But the thing is, the other person also feels the same way.

The best way to get across to someone is to have in mind that facts are never persuasive. If the other person has made up their mind on something, no matter how convincing your points are, you can never get them to agree with you.

Dean J. Arquette

Words That Can Persuade Customers to Visit Your Business

You

Using the word "you" makes whatever you are writing personal. It is one of the easiest ways to persuade your customers. Simply hearing the word "you" has a subtle effect on how your customers react to your requests.

In your writing, this word makes it seem like a conversation on a friendly level.

Free

One word that attracts a lot of people is "free". Who doesn't love to get free stuff?

Providing something for free can influence the decision of an individual. It doesn't matter if there is no change in the actual value of the product.

To understand the power of the word, consider two similar products, like two different brands of cookies. Assume the original price of the first brand, A, is $2 while the other brand, B, is $10. Also, assume that B is a much better option than A.

If there is a sale in which A is going for $1 while B is going for $5, you will notice a lot of customers opting to purchase B. It means that people will prefer to go for superior quality at half the price than low-quality cookies at a meager amount.

Consider another scenario where A is free while B is $4. You will observe that most people will opt for the free option, which is of lower quality.

Now, the thought running through the minds of individuals will be to get a box of cookies at no cost than losing $4 on the same box of cookies. When A becomes free, it becomes more valuable than B, even though there is no change in quality.

This behavior is referred to as loss aversion.

Because

The use of "because" offers a reason why you want someone to do something for you. It is easier to get someone to perform a task if you give them a reason to do so. Following natural human behavior, regardless of how authentic the reason, you can get people to do what you want by adding an idea to your request.

How to Use Because

When conversing with people, using "because" in your sentences is an easy way to persuade them to like you more. Simply make a request or a statement and then connect a reason using "because".

First, create a request or statement.

The following are simple ways to make a request or statement, and then connect them to a reason:

- I would like you to come with me because

- Try this shirt because

- Let's do it at your house because

- I want to go to the concert because

Then, add a reason.

Once you know the request you want to make, the next step is the reason for the request. If you want the reason to work like a charm, it must be convincing. This includes adding a reason that provides specific benefits.

Here are some sentences that show how effective it can be:

- "I hope you will come over to my house."

- Now add a reason to the sentence, and it becomes:

- "I hope you will come over to my house so we can work on the fort."

Including a reason and benefits may look like this:

- "I hope you will come over to my house so we can work on the fort. We will have our private area to hang out once it is complete and you can stay longer without feeling like you are intruding."

You can combine "because" with another crucial persuasive word, such as "you". By combining these two words, you can improve the compelling power of your statements.

There is a reason why these two words are stronger when used together. Using only "because" in a sentence makes the reason for a request objective. To make the reason for a request personal, you must add "you" to the reason.

How Your Business Can Benefit from The Use of Because

The use of 'because' in your business is a simple way to get your customers to comply with your requests. They react instinctively to a request once they hear this powerful word.

As a business, there are times when you will get requests from a customer. In some cases, you may be unable to handle such requests. In your reply to the customer, use this word to explain the reason you are unable to meet the expectations of the customer.

Giving a reason for turning down a job will provide more understanding between you and the customer. It will help maintain a good relationship into the future.

You can also use it to give more insight to your mission. Your goal of setting up a business is not just to make money. There should be a mission that influences business operations. If you can explain your mission and give reasons for the business, you are going to attract more willing sponsors and angel investors.

You can use "because" to explain the reason behind a free product, discount, and special offer. We have all been victim to a hidden catch during some special offers or free product offerings. For this reason, a lot of people are skeptical about taking part. If you want more of your customers or audience to become a part of what you are offering, then give them a clear, honest reason why you are offering free products or discounts.

Explain any issues with product delivery or product damages using the word "because". If your customers will not be getting a product on the promised date, it is their right to know why. You can also make a client more relaxed and understanding when you choose to explain.

It will help prevent requests for refunds since the customers know they will be getting their products.

Instant

Human beings are unpredictable in most situations. In some cases, you may find people looking for delayed gratification while others may prefer instant rewards.

There are different situations where these apply. To become a successful business owner, you will need to understand and accept delayed gratification. You also need to realize that your customers prefer instant rewards.

Certain words stir up the part of the brain that deals with instant rewards. These words include immediately, fast, and instant.

Business owners who are into online product sales can provide instant rewards to their customers with immediate access to the product.

For those that run businesses in the traditional setting, the best way you can provide instant rewards is to deliver the product as soon as possible. In case they make a complaint, you should also get in touch as quickly as you can.

Rapid response can significantly influence the decisions of a customer. There a lot of customers that will not buy your products regularly. Merely including "instant" in a product description can change their opinion.

If you are going to use this word, there is a specific rule you always need to follow. The rule is to ensure that you keep your promise to your customers.

The Social Anxiety and Shyness Solution

If you know you cannot keep a promise, it is better you don't make such a promise. Your customers will be more comfortable if you under-promise but deliver beyond expectations.

Chapter 7:
Get Respect Immediately

The aim of this chapter is to make you become a better person that people will appreciate more. You don't have to be perfect. Everyone makes mistakes. Your ability to own up to your mistakes and care for others are some of the things that earn you respect.

If you are respectful, people will know through your value of yourself, your love for others, your ability to look beyond people's flaws, and your composure. These attributes are respected in any individual.

You want to do unto others the same things you would accept as a person. You will want to be treated with respect and kindness if you are in a pinch. Showing others this type of attitude will make them reciprocate these actions and respect to you.

How to Earn Respect

Your Presentation
This is the easiest way to double the respect you receive.

People are always moved by what they see, and what they hear. Before they get to know your personality, they always get the first impression through your appearance. This is how they will determine if they will accord you respect or not.

What is the best way to present yourself?

Dress to Suit the Occasion

It is quite embarrassing when you are invited to a dinner party, and you dress looking like you are heading to the mall. This speaks volume. You don't have to wear expensive clothes to dress appropriately for an occasion.

All you need to do is to make sure your clothes fit, you look smart, and you look nicely groomed. Consequently, you have given people the impression that you are an upstanding citizen, even before you utter a word.

Some people believe that it is vain to attach any importance to your appearance. This is not true. It is generally advisable not to be excessive about anything, including the way you look, as simplicity gives the aura of sophistication.

This, of course, will involve money (not too much), your ability to take a good bath, have a good hair and body groom (if you are of that type), and looking smart. The simplicity of this trick will get people to respect you.

How You Stand Your Ground on Your Beliefs in A Respectful Way

This scenario presents an opportunity for people to air their differences without offending one another. It is seemingly impossible, as, during the heat of the moment, people are usually not composed. It is utterly wrong to impose your opinion on others. Similarly, it is misguided to reshape your belief to impress people, that is you being disrespectful to yourself.

Take, for instance, you are the only rock lover in the mix of people that prefer classical music. If they gave their opinion on their belief, you will be accorded more respect if you don't impose your belief on them, but generally, agree to disagree about others opinion.

Temperament

If you are easily angered, there is a big possibility that you will not be respected. This is because you will come off as too emotional and irrational. People are more likely to avoid engaging with you in any form of interaction.

It is important to air your opinion, suggestions, or contributions. It is very wrong, however, to be mad if things do not go the way and method you envisage them to be.

There are different ways to approach debatable matters without coming off as angry:

- You should be deliberate or intentional in providing solutions before you engage in a conversation about the problem.

- Things tend to get out of hands quickly when you are in a public environment, so you might want to take the conversation somewhere private.

- Never approach people when you are emotional about something; there is a 70% chance it will go negative. Give it time before you speak.

- Your tone when you talk matters a lot. If you sound accusatory, you might fan a fire to the flame. Instead, construct your words more carefully by using statements like, "I believe you don't..." rather than saying, "You never go out of your way..."

- It always pays to be composed and collected.

- Try to exercise empathy. This way, you put yourself in the other person's situation, and you might relate better to the circumstances.

- Never be on the defensive. Admit when you are wrong.

If you can successfully remain calm through things, people will trust you to handle situations and will respect you.

Acknowledge Your Mistakes

This might not be a popular trick, but it brings results. People who refuse to own up to their mistakes are considered prideful. To be prideful means you believe you are better than others. This does great harm to any relationship.

Here is an example of a scenario. Imagine a friend's mistake cost you money and instead of owning up to it, they try to justify it. They continuously display this bad behavioral pattern. Such persons will quickly lose any form of respect from his/her peers.

To be prideful is not an appealing attribute in a person, and this can cost you good relationships, be it business, personal, or casual. To earn respect from people, it is advisable to be humble. Nobody is known to be perfect, and as a result, people relate more to you when you admit your wrongs and consider your mistakes.

If you can't think about what to say when you make mistakes, start by saying this, "I am so sorry I came off as offensive, not my best attribute, it won't happen again," or you can say, "I apologize for the wrong I have done." Very easy!

Owning up to your mistakes gives you respect and doesn't make you seem like a difficult person to deal with. This will go a long way in strengthening your relationship with others, as they will feel appreciated and relevant

How You Respect Others to Get Respect

To be respected, you also must respect others. Respecting the next person has a significant impact. Don't limit your respect to people of high influence or positions of importance.

Respect should come from a more natural ground. As humans, the end goal in life usually is to attain a place of peace, happiness, and wealth. We are all going through a different route to accomplish that.

So, irrespective of one's opinion or belief, at the end of the day, we all want the same thing. Instead of treating people cruelly because they don't fit your definition or standard of anything, it is better to extend an act of kindness and genuine love.

You may wonder how this relates to earning respect. If you are to describe the most disrespectful people you have ever come across, it will be those who felt they were better than others, either because of their wealth, position, race, beliefs, or class. It always goes back to being full of pride. These are the people that get the least amount of respect.

Act in A Respectful Manner

Being respectful goes way beyond words; it is also how you act. Your body language can show that you are disrespectful. For instance, your boss is talking to you, and you don't give him your attention. Instead, you are concentrating on your laptop screen. That is considered rude, or if you roll your eyes or walk away during a conversation.

There are various attributes that can show how disrespectful you are to a person. Agreement is not the only sign of respect. Differing opinions makes us unique.

If you are known to act in ways and manners that are considered disrespectful, people will generally want to avoid you, and that can create damage to your relationships.

Stop Insulting Others

To act in a disrespectful manner is not only when you are addressing the person himself, but it could also be you talking bad about another person without them being present. This act is rampant in social gatherings, workplaces, and organizations.

The person you are talking to will never respect you. They are most times careful, knowing that you will probably talk about them in the same manner as well. You are termed as the gossip and the one who creates rifts between people.

To earn respect, you need to be an open person. Don't talk bad about people. That way, you are considered trustworthy and respected.

How to Handle People Taking You for Granted?

If you feel like people often get to know you so they can exploit you, then you really need to go through this section with full attention.

The best way to prevent people from taking you for granted is to set boundaries and stick to them. This tells people that you would not tolerate them taking you for granted and that you deserve to be respected.

Before you set your boundaries, you need to consider those things you can control.

Do not set boundaries you cannot enforce. For instance, you have friends who continuously loan money from you but never bother to pay you back because they probably feel you can afford to let it go. You can decide to limit the amount of money you give out to them on loan or make them sign an undertaking to pay you back.

It is also important to tell the person who is guilty of such acts. This is because people have a reason for how they act the way they do. Hearing from them will help you to assess how best to enforce your boundaries. You can also figure out ways to help them out without giving them room to take advantage of you.

For instance, ask them when they intend to pay you back and insist, they pay you back before loaning them more money. Setting boundaries does not mean they will not be crossed. As humans, doing things in the same manner repeatedly can make it seem like there is nothing wrong.

When this happens, the next action to take is to talk about it again with them. Make them understand:

- That you do not like their actions

- What your boundaries are

- The reason why you chose to set those boundaries

If they keep violating your boundaries, then you need to take drastic actions to bring about the changes you desire. The sad truth is that you might have to cut yourself off from them to maintain peace.

A lot of people who find it difficult to command respect from others feel like nobody ever listens to them.

- Do people overlook your opinions, or do you feel like no one takes you seriously?

- Are you constantly being interrupted or ignored?

- Is no one listening while you are speaking?

Your presence will be felt, and you are heard when you apply the tips below. These tips will make people have more respect for you. Tips on how to speak so people will listen to you include the following:

- Address people by their names during a conversation.

- Avoid talking in parables or using jaw-breaking words for easy comprehension. People will tend to keep away from you if they struggle through understanding what you are saying.

- Let your conversations also involve the other person's interests. Do not make the mistake of talking about only your interests.

- Gesticulate more often to drive your point across and keep their interest.

- Ask the other person a few questions. It makes them more involved and interested in the conversation.

- Do not avoid eye contact. Making eye contact with a person during a conversation shows them how interested you are in the conversation. If it is a group conversation, give everyone equal eye contacts to make everyone feel valued.

- Work on making your voice clearer and more audible for everyone to hear.

- Complaints and negativity should be minimized. Otherwise, people will lose interest in talking to you.

- Avoid bragging. No matter how hard you try to conceal it, people will see through you and keep their distance.

- Ask people how they think you can improve your communication skills.

- Use effective pauses. Silence sometimes plays an important role in communication.

- Change your tone and speed when talking. This has a way of making the conversation lively. You can practice this at home before trying it out in public.

Get Respect with Your Body Language

Body language can describe how a person feels about himself even without saying it.

You will come off as shy or insecure if you continuously walk around with your eyes fixed on the ground and your shoulders hunched. You will barely be respected with such body language.

If you walk around with your head held high, you portray confidence. People will respect you because you respect yourself and they sometimes believe that you have something worth being proud of. Below are some characteristics of confident body language:

- Walking with a purpose

- Good eye contact during a conversation or when addressing a group of people

- Good posture, avoiding slouching or crossing of your arms

- Gesticulate more often when speaking

- Keep your chin up and eyes forward instead of looking down

Always remember that there is a difference between confidence and arrogance. Arrogance rids a person of respect.

Chapter 8:
How to Analyze People

For one to decipher the hints people give off, either spoken or unspoken, one must see beyond the facade. It is impossible to know the entire story of anyone through rational thinking. To properly analyze an individual, you must become knowledgeable on other means of human communication such as body language.

It is also required that you let go of any preconceived ideas, sentiments (like indignations), or any reservations that could cloud your vision of people. The most important thing is to stay open-minded and absorb knowledge without bias.

It doesn't matter if the subject of study is your superior, colleague, or companion; it is crucial that you remain neutral and open-minded to get a correct result. Also, you need to discard any previous belief you may have about a person in order to perform a great analysis. Those who study people are taught to study even the latent. They know how to use the essential senses which help them to see beyond what is typically seen in order to properly analyze an individual.

What Is Body Language?
This is a type of communication which is nonverbal. It is dependent on the various movements of the body including minor and major

movements. These minor and major body movements include changes in facial expressions, posture, and gestures.

Sometimes, the use of body language may be in combination with speech, or in other cases it may replace the use of speech. Body language can be used in a conscious or subconscious manner.

What Does Body Language Tell You About A Person?

Although speech may be your most important means of communication now, you used body language for communication when you were younger.

Understanding the message an individual is trying to pass is often dependent on your ability to analyze the body language of the individual. You may be able to assess if a person is lying or if they are trying to gain more understanding of a presentation.

Below are some easy ways that body language can help you understand the emotions of an individual:

Determining A Lie or Anxiousness in An Individual

In western cultures, a clear sign of nervousness is the inability of an individual to make eye contact. It may also signify fear or nervousness.

An individual that is not confident in the information they are giving will typically try to cover their mouth or eyes while speaking.

Lack of self-assurance will often lead to anxiousness. There are other apparent indications of anxiousness, and they include sweating, licking of the lips, and shaking.

It Shows Interest

Body language that indicates interest includes proper eye contact and nodding. A person that is interested in the topic of discussion will avoid fiddling with a pen, checking the time, or using their smartphone.

It is essential you don't mistake someone who is listening passively for an active listener. A passive listener will not be able to attain any of the information you are trying to convey. A proactive body language is also a good indication of a person paying attention to you.

It Is an Excellent Means of Identifying A Bored Individual

Depending on the body language of an individual, it is possible to determine if they are bored or not. There is one significant reason why it is difficult for an individual to mask boredom. It is because their desires do not align with their experiences now.

A person who is successful will possess charisma, energy, and strong body language. In addition to all these qualities, this individual will also know how to maintain eye contact. Combining all these qualities will make an individual capable of using body language to communicate with others effectively.

You will notice that such an individual will be in total control of the gestures they make while speaking and will also be capable of drawing the attention of others. If you can meet such an individual, you will be able to sense their confidence through the perfect handshake.

It Is an Easy Way to Identify Submission

Signs of helplessness from an individual can imply that the person is submissive. Such a person will often have their head downwards. Nervousness and an active effort to avoid criticism and conflict are signs of submissiveness. A face that is devoid of emotion also helps to prevent drawing too much attention.

Analyzing Body Language

As a form of nonverbal communication, body language replaces the use of words with physical motions. The physical actions are used to express the necessary information.

Gestures, facial expressions, body posture, touch, and eye movement are some of the physical motions that help in analyzing body language.

Analysis and interpretation of the body language of human beings are known as kinesics. Sign language is not the same as body language. There are significant differences between sign language and body language.

The features of sign language include grammar systems and other properties that are present in other standard languages. There is no grammar system in body language, and there is no general interpretation of body movements.

What Is Nonverbal Communication?

Nonverbal communication is a method of communication that doesn't depend on the use of words. There are similarities between nonverbal communication and body language. Body language is a branch of nonverbal communication.

People can use nonverbal communication in various ways including the following:

- Speech rate

- Personal space
- Hairstyle
- Touch
- Volume of voice
- Gestures
- Clothes
- Facial expressions
- Hygiene

The Role of Nonverbal Communication

The role of nonverbal communication in the life of an individual is often undermined. This is a skill that assists individuals in relating to others. Your nonverbal communication skills often determine your ability to solidify your relationships with others.

Different cultures interpret nonverbal communication in various ways. In some cases, the lack of a nonverbal communication cue has a specific meaning.

In nonverbal communication, each movement and combination of various movements such as eye movement, facial expressions, hand gestures, and postures has a meaning. Nonverbal communication cues may either be subtle or overt. Depending on how it is used, it is open to misinterpretation.

It is one of the easiest ways to assess the emotions of an individual. A person that intends to be deceptive will often make a nonverbal communication cue that has a meaning different from their body language. It is because nonverbal communication is not easy to fake.

Types of Nonverbal Communication

Nonverbal communication is present in different forms. The way people interpret nonverbal communication will vary for everyone. The message they pass regarding the thoughts of an individual is also broad.

The different types of nonverbal communication you will experience daily include the following:

- Eye movement and contact that represent the direction of a person's eyes

- Facial expressions that represent changes in features of the face

- Posture indicates the body of an individual as it relates to the body of other individuals

- Body movements that show how the body of an individual moves

- Tone of voice is an indication of the variance in voice pitch, such as the use of sarcasm

- Gestures that signify the movement of the head and limbs

Nonverbal communication is essential to emphasize, support, or contradict a verbal message.

Importance of Nonverbal Communication

When running a business or making new relationships, understanding and analyzing nonverbal communication can give you an upper hand. Using your knowledge of nonverbal communication, it is possible to investigate the reactions of clients and what influences their decisions.

If you can read nonverbal communications quickly, it is possible to avoid making any mistakes in front of clients, coworkers, family, or friends.

Ways of Analyzing People

The first way has to do with hints given off by body language.

It has been discovered that words make up for about seven percent of communication, while body language makes up fifty-five percent, and tone of voice is responsible for the remaining thirty percent. For this, it is pertinent to let the art of analyzing body language hi come naturally to you. Don't force it or get logical, be calm and let it flow. Be at ease, relax, and pay attention.

Be Observant of People's Outlook

There are key things to observe when analyzing people which include what they are wearing, how they are dressed, what their dress sense depicts. Each dress sense could be a sign of casualty, ambition, sexuality, or spirituality.

Be Attentive to Poses

There are questions to ask yourself concerning the posture of people, which are: Do they exude confidence with the way they raise their heads? Do they carry themselves with an unsure posture or fidget, which could mean their self-worth is low? Are their chests pushed out, which could mean arrogance or pride?

Pay Attention to Shifts in Body Parts

Bending and Space
People naturally stay close to people they like as opposed to the people they don't like. It is important to take note of a person's proximity to others.

Folded Arms and Legs
This posture portrays annoyance, self-justification, or self-defense. The crossing of the legs is usually accompanied by pointed toes in the direction of another person of interest.

Concealed Hands
Hands on laps, in pockets, or at the rear is usually a sign of people keeping a secret.

Biting of The Lip or Picking of The Finger Nails
This is usually a sign that people are anxious about something, or they are in a compromising position. These acts serve as an avenue for relief.

Decode Countenance
Feelings of people can easily be displayed on people's faces. One is assumed to be worried or of an overthinking nature with the appearance of deep frown lines on the face. Laugh lines depict happiness.

Puckered lips portray annoyance, resentment, or disdain. Grinding of the teeth and jaw clenching portray anxiety.

The second way has to do with listening to your instincts.

Aligning with people is not just about words or body language; instincts take you a step further. Being intuitive requires your guts rather than what is on your mind. It helps in better identifying and analyzing every unspoken word by paying attention to depictions, sounds accidentally let off, or expressions, instead of relying on rational thinking.

What helps when getting to know someone deeply other than what's beneath their facade is your instinct, which enables you to go beyond what can be seen physically to obtain a desirable result.

List of Instinctive Hints

Acknowledge Insight
These bursts of visions come so quickly when discussing with people that it might be easy to overlook them and replace them with other thoughts in an instant. It helps to be sensitive, so you don't miss out on them.

Respect Your Instincts
That initial awakening you get during a new connection, even before you have the chance of gathering your thoughts is your instinct tugging at you. It suggests inner peace or discomfort to you. These emotions happen quickly and help you measure the sincerity of people upon first contact.

Be on Guard for Impulsive Compassion

Take note of your emotions when studying people. Your emotions can get so intense that you begin to experience the same emotions your subject is exhibiting. Be sensitive to how you feel after each session with people. Check if you experience body pains or feel downtrodden. A professional examination is necessary to be sure you are empathetic.

Goose Pimples Sensitivity

That mild stinging sensation we get when we meet those we look up to or when they say something, we can relate to is known as goose pimples. They also occur when you sense that you know someone even though they have never crossed your path.

A Third Way of Analyzing People: Respond to Strong Feelings

Feelings resonate well with our instincts, and one of the ways we get sensitive around people is through feelings. While being around some people can put you at ease, being around some others could be exhausting; it makes you want to look for a way out. This careful nudge is usually sensed somewhere around the body although it can't be seen. Medically, it is called "chi" in Chinese, a sensation that is very important to overall health.

Tactics for Studying Strong Feelings

Be Aware of People's Presence

This does not necessarily have anything to do with words or actions; it is the energy we generally give off. It hangs over us like a cloud. When analyzing people, pay attention to nature. Do they have an attractive nature? This does not necessarily have anything to do with words or actions; it is the energy people generally give off.

Pay Attention to How People Sound and Their Laughter

Feelings can be deduced from how loudly or softly we speak, or how we otherwise sound. Variations in sound make up a reverberation. Be observant of how the sound of people's voices makes you feel as you study them. Are their voices relaxing or calm? Do they sound harsh, resentful, or fretful?

Be Observant of People's Eyes

The eyes tell you a lot of things if you pay attention to them. It has been discovered that the eyes send a lot of signals just like the brain does to the body. Pay close attention to the eyes of people and look out for what they are saying. Do they look sensual? Calm? Are they filled with rage? Do they express cruelty? Also, can you decipher a love life from those eyes? Or are they evasive?

Observe the Response to Body Contact

Body contact can cause us to emit strong emotions that feel like a surge of energy. Be aware of how a handshake or a hug makes you feel. Do you feel relaxed, or uncomfortable? Does the person's hand feel damp, which could signify agitation, or does it feel flaccid, which could signify distraction or inferiority?

Chapter 9:
How to Think Under Pressure and Crush It

There are different times when we find ourselves under pressure. It may be the moment after your presentation when you must answer questions. The same also applies to selling a product to a prospective buyer.

To be successful under pressure, you must think of ways to pass your message across clearly. You must be confident. Having adequate knowledge can also help you to get through a high-pressure situation.

Learning to think on your feet is one of the few techniques that can get you to overcome any high-pressure situation. Below are some of the methods you can implement:

Avoid Jumping into Your Response

One of the mistakes people make in a high-pressure situation is responding too soon. It is often due to anxiety. As a result, they begin the response without a clear idea of where it will lead.

To give the best response when under pressure, you can start by taking a deep breath. It is a technique that provides an opening for you to put your thoughts in order. It works in both conversations and in interview settings.

Since you are taking your time to give an appropriate response, you also reduce the chances of getting flustered.

Ensure That Your Body Is Functioning at Its Normal Pace

A simple sign that you are under pressure is an increase in your heart rate. Your speech is also much faster than normal, and your brain will also be performing faster than usual.

A combination of these is sure to have a negative impact. If your brain is working at a faster pace, it means you are generating thoughts faster than you can analyze them. With an increase in the rate at which you speak, you may end up saying things that may make you seem weird or get you into trouble.

By slowing down the pace of your speech, your brain will be able to plan how you should present your thoughts accurately.

Develop A Concise Response Based on The Question

If someone is asking you a question, the answer that the person is expecting should be specific. The problem with answering under pressure is that you may end up giving answers that contain excess information, or answers with minimal information. Each answer has its demerits.

If the response contains too much information, you may take a long time to answer. People quickly lose interest once a reply starts getting too long. In addition to blurting out things that should be kept secret, people will see you as a blabbermouth who is also boring.

A short answer also has its downsides. If you are trying to get out of a high-pressure situation, short answers will only lead to more questions. Since this type of answer will not reveal the necessary information, you are giving the other person full control of how the conversation should go.

To deal with these issues, giving a concise answer is best. Such an answer will be short enough to reveal the answer to the question and avoid giving out too much information. To develop the perfect answer, you must ensure that you are focusing on only what the question has asked.

There will be so much information available in the form of thoughts, but you need to select only what is most important. Attaching a supporting fact to the response is another excellent way to give more insight.

Stalling

The response to some questions requires more than a deep breath to formulate. In such cases, there are specific tactics you can implement to stall for time. Below are some of the tactics you can apply to get more time to think of a proper response:

Create A Focus

Some questions may have a vast scope. A good tactic is to narrow the question down to a smaller scope. This will make it easier to answer the question.

Request for A Definition of Terms

Some questions may contain terminology that you are unfamiliar with. Before you start coming up with an answer, ask that the other person define these terminologies. You are only doing this to make sure that your answer will align with what they want to hear.

Say the Question to Yourself

As you repeat a question you are asked, you will be able to gain clarity on certain parts of the issue. You can rearticulate the question to make it simpler for you to tackle.

Practice Various Questions That Cause High-Pressure

Specific questions commonly come up in high-pressure situations. Practicing such questions will help in developing better ways to answer such questions.

The questions in this list may differ for each workplace environment, business, or friends circle. Identifying questions that cause an increase in the pace of your speech and your thinking is essential.

Sometimes, a person merely asking how your business is doing may put you in a high-pressure situation. It may also be a question about your vision for the business.

Don't Take A Defensive Position

High-pressure situations often put you in a defensive position. There are various reasons why you may want to get into a defensive position. It is often due to criticisms.

If you come up with a proposal or a strategy for growth, it is often a good idea to have someone look at the strategy or proposal. Anyone looking at your documents may have found some areas where you have made certain errors. Getting criticism for such mistakes may often cause you to take the defensive position.

A typical reply to criticism that shows you have taken a defensive position is the use of, "No, but..." as your response. A better reply that gives room for creative thinking and sharing ideas is to reply with, "Yes, and..."

Make Moments Where You Are Under Pressure Seem Like Fun

The way you look at a high-pressure situation will affect how you perform. If your interpretation of a high-pressure situation is terrible, then you will have issues dealing with it.

The same also applies if you see such a situation as a threat. Your interpretation of this situation will lead you to a place of fear and result in a loss of self-confidence. Fear, in this case, can interfere with your judgment, thought process, and memory. It is what causes you to act on impulse.

Change your view of a high-pressure situation. Consider it a fun challenge you need to overcome. As a result of your new outlook, you can eliminate fear and gain more control of the situation.

Falling Apart Under Pressure

When you find yourself under pressure, certain things may cause you to fall apart. If you find yourself in a situation like a previous moment when you failed, you may begin to worry. It is normal human behavior to worry about failing again and making the wrong choice. If you are not careful, you may end up overthinking every decision.

It doesn't matter how well you usually perform a task. Once you start overthinking, it will cripple your ability to work effectively. It will often result in your inability to take a step forward.

When you want to avoid failure, it is common to keep telling yourself not to fail. If only you understood that this action only increases the chances of doing whatever you are trying to avoid. Also, you also lose a lot of willpower in the process.

Dean J. Arquette

Merely focusing on the task at hand is an easy way to avoid failure when you are under pressure. If you are in a high-pressure situation but retain your positive outlook, you can see the case as a challenge you need to overcome.

Chapter 10:
How to Sell Anything to Anyone All the Time

The growth of your business often depends on your ability to sell your products to your customers. The truth is that not everyone is a great salesperson. Nonetheless, you can train yourself to become better at selling anything to anyone.

One of the great things about making sales on your own is that you are in control of your business growth. Your profits at the end of the month are often a reflection of your sales performance during the month. As a result, you can assess your skills and appreciate your efforts more.

To ensure you are making enormous profits at the end of each month, you need to develop yourself. There are specific methods and techniques you can implement to get better at selling anything to anyone.

Below are some methods you can follow:

Show That You Are an Authority
Solidifying your position as an authority in a niche is the easiest way to sell your products to people. It is the same reason why consumers are willing to spend thousands of dollars on an iPhone or a Samsung device.

Have people seen a demonstration of your knowledge or skills? Is there a reason for people to trust your words?

If you can solidify your image as an authority in your target market, it becomes easier to get people to buy from you. Product sales are often dependent on trust. Your customers are sure to keep buying your products if you can make them trust you explicitly.

Becoming an authority in a specific niche has never been as easy as it is in recent times. Access to social media offers you the opportunity to share relevant information and create quality content. Blogs also have a significant impact depending on how you use them.

Connect with Your Customers

A lot of sales are often a result of the connection between the seller and the buyer. It may not be due to the quality of the product available. Making sales will be easy if you have the best product on the market, but customers will be more willing to buy from a seller they feel is like them in many ways.

Forming a connection with your customers is quite easy. You need to connect on an emotional level. Your use of words, analogies, and anecdotes can be of immense help. When people decide to purchase a product, their emotions often cloud their logical reasoning. Things like a simple greeting and compliments go a long way when connecting with a customer.

Comprehensive market research can set you up for great relationships with customers. It also helps you to create a profile of the customer you are meeting for the first time. Following the results of your market research, it is easy to identify the problems your customers face, and the solution to these problems.

Making sales is essential, but being human comes first. It is important you show your human side before trying to make sales.

Don't Be Obnoxious

Just because you are trying to sell your product doesn't mean you should become intolerable. Your first impression on your prospective buyers matters a lot. Don't be the blabbermouth during the conversation.

You should have a filter for anything you say to your prospect. This filter should help decide what information is relevant to the prospect and what is not.

Let the focus of the conversation be your buyer. Tailor the interaction to revolve around the buyer. This extends to any voicemails you leave, any emails you send, and more.

Emotions are important

When trying to make sales, a lot of people underestimate the impact of emotions. We often place our hopes on prospective customers making decisions based on logic. This is not true in most cases.

Making decisions based on emotions is what makes customer behavior very unpredictable. If you are unable to take the emotions of your customers into account, you won't be able to make consistent sales.

To make the most of the emotions, the first step is to understand the various emotions that can influence a decision. They include the following:

- Pride

- Anger

- Greed

- Shame

- Fear

- Joy

During your conversation with a prospect, you may be able to draw out certain emotions. Connecting with a prospect will make them happy. It then results in an emotional bias during the decision-making process.

To make sure you can make sales whenever you want, you should be able to influence at least two positive emotions in a prospect. It should be done subtly, without the prospect noticing. If you draw out too many emotions, both positive and negative, you will end up compounding the process.

Not All Customers Are Good for You

A good salesperson always ensures that their impact on the customer will make them return another time. Nonetheless, it is vital you understand that not all customers are good for the business.

There are specific interactions with customers that will turn out badly no matter how hard you try. The earlier you understand this, the better it will be. Keeping a lousy customer around will have a negative influence on you, other customers, and the business.

You may find yourself in a dicey situation sometimes. The customer that may be ruining your brand may be your highest-paying customer. It is for situations like this that you need to come up with new ideas each day.

What Value Are You Selling?

Customers usually have an interest in the value a product offers. The cost is what makes the product unique. That is how you survive the competition.

The value of your product can also be the dream that you are selling. In some cases, it may be an opportunity for your customers to turn in more profits.

Explaining the value of a product to a customer before trying to sell the product will have a positive impact. You are giving the customers time to visualize the outcomes and opportunities they can get from the product.

If you rush into trying to sell your product, it will take less than 5 seconds for a customer to assess the product thoroughly. It is not enough time for them to get a good understanding of the product.

A product value that promises high returns on investment is always attractive to customers.

Do Your Research but Remain an Active Listener?

Getting information on your prospects is a lot easier with social media. It is the least you can do if you expect your prospects to also learn about your products.

Various social media platforms make it easy to do your research. They include the following:

- Facebook
- LinkedIn
- Blogs
- Google
- Twitter

Performing your research provides all the information you need regarding a prospect. It doesn't mean you will get all the information you need.

To fill in the gaps of your information, you need to remain an active listener. If you ask critical questions, you can get the relevant answers from your prospects. It is then possible to better understand their problem and proffer the best solution.

Come up with a list of questions to ask your prospects before you meet. These are to serve as a guide. You don't have to force the conversation.

As an active listener, remain quiet while your prospect answers each question. Don't ask too many questions at once. You want to get as much information as possible.

Create A Profile of Your Prospect

There are lots of reasons why a profile is essential if you want to make sales. A profile helps you identify what products meet the requirements of a prospect.

If you want to be able to sell anything to anyone, you need to understand that not everything is suitable for everyone.

In selling anything to anyone, you must define the prospect that fits into your definition of "anyone". Once you define this prospect, you can manage your time and increase your chances of successfully closing a sale.

Set Your Mind on Closing the Sale

From the moment you meet a prospect, your mind should already be on closing the sale. A sale is not complete unless you can close it. Everything you are trying to do is for this final moment.

You can significantly improve your chances of closing a sale if you are consciously working towards it. This is the moment when you make the sale, so it is vital. It is also vital you learn how to close a sale to increase your success rate.

How to Close A Sale?

Closing a sale involves negotiating the best deal for your product. It is a skill that you master through practice. The only way you will get practice is to close sales with your customers frequently.

As you develop your skills as a negotiator, you will become more assertive and tactful when dealing with your customers. It doesn't matter if you are not a natural at negotiating; the potential is present in everyone.

Specific tips can help you develop your negotiating skills to make you better at closing sales. Below are the essential tips you need:

Prepare for The Process

There are some necessary steps we often take for granted. Preparation is often one of those steps. It is easy to overlook this step when you feel you have all the necessary information you need.

To boost your chances when trying to close a deal, you need to know everything about your customer. It is also crucial you identify the services and products that align with their needs.

Due diligence is critical in this situation. It is through this process you can determine the amount your prospect is willing to spend on the product. Personal information on your customer can also be helpful. This may be the area they live, favorite restaurants, and other preferences that can help gain trust when you mix it in subtly during the conversation.

Research on other products available on the market can also help you determine your product information that should remain a secret until trying to make the sale. Dropping such information as a surprise is sure to throw the customer off balance, which you can use to your advantage. It makes it easier to close the deal.

Create A Balance Between Being Nice and Being Firm

If you are not willing to compromise at some points, you may end up losing the sale. As a negotiator, understanding situations that require firmness and those that require you to be nice.

Why is this important? Closing a sale is not the end of your business with a customer. You always want customers to come back another time. Being nice while trying to close a sale will ensure that your relationship with a customer remains positive.

Your Body Language and Tone

During a conversation, your body language always speaks the loudest. Combining your body language with an excellent tone of voice will set the mood for a great conversation. A lot of the messages that you wish to pass across during a conversation is often done using body language.

Body language and tone of voice in a formal environment is usually different from what you use when trying to make a customer feel comfortable. You need to smile more and try to talk at a much slower pace.

Don't Undersell

It can be difficult to get a good deal when negotiating with a customer that has more experience. Sometimes, you end up making the wrong decisions. This may be to avoid getting rejected.

A counter-offer is usually necessary after a customer refuses to accept your terms. To make a suitable counter-offer, it is vital you ask the customer for an explanation. The explanation should give you clear reasons why they are not accepting your terms. You can then create a counter-offer that is beneficial to both you and the customer.

In some cases, it is better to have the client come up with the counter-offer. Remaining silent after a refusal will often prompt a counter-offer from the customer.

Avoid Giving the Initial Offer

A good thing about closing a deal with a customer is the limitless opportunities that are available. A simple step that opens the door of opportunities is to avoid making the first offer.

If your customer makes the first offer on what you are selling, you have a higher chance of receiving a great deal. As a good negotiator, you will still make a counter-offer at a higher price.

After a period during which there will have been various counter-offers, you will be able to settle on a price that provides an excellent return on investment (ROI).

Learn to Manage Your Time Wisely

If you want to make lots of sales, you should know how to manage your time effectively. To manage your time, you should be able to tell if a person is going to buy your product or not.

You should also have a limit on the amount of time you spend with one customer. Taking too much time talking to a single customer will eat into the time you would have spent convincing another prospect.

To be successful in making sales, you should be able to determine a prospect that will buy your product within the first minute of your interaction. In most cases, when a customer starts asking too many questions, it is often a sign that they have no interest in making a purchase.

You can also observe the trends in your previous sales attempt. You may notice that it has been difficult making sales after four minutes of conversing with a prospect. In future interactions, you can set your limit to four minutes. As soon as this time elapses, you know it is profitable to move on to the next prospect.

Implementing Psychological Tricks

If you are trying to sell something to someone, there are certain tricks that can influence the response of the other individual. Using these tricks effectively will have an impact on your sales.

Some of the psychological tricks you should know include the following:

Confirmation Bias

This implies that people will choose a piece of information that is like their belief rather than another option with accurate facts.

Rhyme-As-Reason Effect

People tend to accept rhyming sentences as facts compared to sentences that do not rhyme.

Decoy Effect

If you have two options you want people to choose from, adding a third option can improve the possibility of your customers picking one of the two real options. The third option usually has some benefits over the first option but is inferior to the second option.

Peak-End Rule

If you decide to make a presentation, a high point during the presentation and the end of the presentation remain fresh in the memories of your listeners.

Anchoring Effect

People use the initial information they get to compare any other information they receive about the product.

Dean J. Arquette

Sales Techniques You Should Know

Use the Silent Treatment

Silence when trying to make a sale is a powerful tool that can work for you or against you. The silence can make people feel very uncomfortable, and that makes customers make decisions in your favor. To take advantage of this technique, you must be strong willed. If you end up breaking the silence, you may end up underselling. Merely state your price and go quiet. Now, wait for your customer to break the silence.

The Free Trial Technique

This is a popular technique in making sales. It is suitable for both online and traditional sales methods. It allows the customer to get a feel of the product and its features before they decide to purchase.

There are different ways through which you can apply the free trial technique. You can choose to run a 3-day trial for free or offer a money back guarantee for a certain duration. As customers get attached to the product, it becomes more difficult to send it back.

Through the free trial, customers can assess the functionality of the product you are selling. There are a few skin care products that offer 30-day money back guarantees. If you don't notice any significant improvement in your skin while using the product, you can return it for a refund.

If you offer music tutorials online, you may decide to offer a 7-day free trial period. It gives your customers the time to assess your teaching and how much they gain during this time.

Using Offers and Discounts to Promote Sales

This is another technique that a lot of sellers use. You can also observe it on Amazon. Discounts are also available when buying from street vendors. It may be difficult to notice because you must work for your discount by bargaining.

In supermarkets, grocery stores, and online stores, you can find some discounted products at a very high price. The discount will make the deal very attractive and almost impossible to pass up. This is when a lot of people give in to impulse spending habits.

Implementing offers is another excellent way to make it difficult for customers not to purchase your product. You can create an offer by including another product whenever a customer purchases your product. It is also possible to invest in a sales promotion, such as a Christmas sales promo, or Black Friday sales.

Scarcity Marketing

Scarcity refers to the unavailability of a product. If you need a product but cannot find it anywhere, then it is scarce. Scarcity marketing is a technique that prompts customers to make immediate purchases.

The trick behind the effectiveness of this simple strategy is how it works on the minds of buyers. Customers believe that if they fail to take advantage of the opportunity at that moment, they may never get the chance again. As a result, sales increase when a product is scarce.

In some cases, a ban on imports on a commodity will cause customers to stock up on that commodity.

There are different ways you can implement scarcity marketing. Labeling a product as an "Exclusive Product" or a "Limited Edition" is a form of scarcity marketing. It may not look like a scarcity marketing strategy, but customers react because they don't want to miss out on this deal.

You can better understand how to implement scarcity marketing strategies below:

Rare Items

If you are a seller of rare items, then you will always find collectors who are willing to pay a reasonable price for your products. Any rare item is unique and almost impossible to find. It can be the original edition of a favorite book or a coin from the 18th century.

The thought of being one of the few people in the world to own an item often prompts customers to purchase rare items.

Limited Quantity Products

Any product available in limited quantity means that only a specific number of these products were made. Also, the company will not manufacture this product at any time in the future.

Other limited quantity products are only available depending on the season. Limited quantity products may be a remastered game or a game console with a unique design that differs from the original.

Chapter 11:
Use Psychology to Get What You Want

Persuading someone to do what you want is a process that must be subtle. This makes it a bit complex to achieve unless you can harness the right skills. If you lack basic persuasion skills, it may be difficult to get someone to do something as easy as lending you a pen.

There are various tricks you can use in getting people to do what you want. These tricks will help improve your ability to sway opinions in your favor.

Psychology is an area that provides all the necessary tips and tricks that help in persuading others. If you know how to influence the function of the brain, it is possible to get people to do what you want.

Politicians and salespeople are a part of many individuals who have discovered easy methods of swaying opinions. It is the same way a company advertises a new product and convinces its customers of the benefits of that product.

What are some of the psychological tricks you can use? Below are some of these excellent tricks.

The Bandwagon Effect
It is easier to get someone to accept a belief if there are lots of other people who also accept this belief. This is what the bandwagon effect

describes. Just because people accept this belief does not imply that it is the right belief.

By implementing this psychological trick, you can persuade people to do something you want. The first step is to get a few people to accept or do whatever task you need. These may be your friends or family members.

Once you have people who are doing the task, you can then easily persuade another person to join in. If you are trying to sell a product, you can give your friends and family free products to try out. When your prospect sees others who use your products, it becomes easier to get them to buy the product.

Priming

This is a technique that can subtly influence the decision-making process of an individual. There are different types of priming. Some of the most accessible types of priming you can use to get what you want include repetition priming, associative priming, and conceptual priming.

Associative priming is the use of an object that is closely associated with another object. By introducing the first object, it triggers the memory of the individual to another similar object.

Conceptual priming involves the use of a stimulus that has a conceptual relationship with the response. An example of objects in the same conceptual category will be a gaming console and a gamepad.

Repetition priming is the use of a specific stimulus to prompt a response at a faster rate. The faster response is due to the repetitive pairing of the same stimulus and response. An example will be asking an individual to repeat the word 'silk' ten times and then asking, "what do cows drink?" Due to the repetition of the word silk, the fastest response to the question will be milk.

The priming process of an individual is usually subtle and impossible to notice. Priming an individual to make a decision that will benefit you is quite easy if you set up the environment properly. If you want someone to decide to eat a bowl of cereal in the morning, placing a bowl, a milk jug, and a cereal carton will make the decision easy for them to make.

Don't Say A Word

This is very effective if you are trying to get information out of an individual. If you ask a question, you might get an unsatisfactory answer. Just saying nothing and staring will often get the individual to keep talking.

It is essential you maintain eye contact while remaining silent. If you are lucky, you may get the person to tell the truth about a situation. However, the direct eye contact and the pause can often be misinterpreted as you already having the accurate information.

Use Tiredness to Your Advantage

Tiredness can affect people both mentally and physically. At this point, you can quickly get what you want out of an individual. A good time to use this trick is after a workday.

If you have a demand or request, you can put it across at this moment when they are not mentally alert. Due to their level of tiredness, they will lack the energy to argue with you over these requests.

Contrasting

This is a technique that a lot of people know about. When you want to get something from someone, you start by asking for something bigger than your real request. Since the demand is too high, there will be a need to lower your demand.

While you negotiate with the other person, you will reach an agreement of lower demand. While this will appear as a win for the other person, you know that you have obtained your original demand.

Reciprocity Norm

The reciprocity norm is a simple trick that has been in existence for a very long time. It is the primary desire of humans to repay their debt to others. It implies that you will be more inclined to help someone if they have been of help to you in the past.

Now that you understand this simple trick, how can you make it work for you?

It is straightforward. If you want to get someone to do something for you, do something nice for the person first. You don't have to go overboard; a simple box of doughnuts will suffice.

As a result of your kind gesture, they will be willing to accept a request from you when the opportunity arises.

Show Them What They Stand to Gain

When bargaining with someone, getting them to focus on what they will gain will make it easier to influence their decision. The way you phrase your sentences is vital in this situation. Let the emphasis be on what they will receive and not what they will lose.

When phrasing your sentence, your offer should come first before your demand. It should look like you are providing something of value so you can get their attention. Once they show interest, you can then make your request.

Let People Watch

It is easy to persuade someone if there are other people around watching. This is only effective if you are persuading them to do something that is right. It is a technique that works almost all the time.

If it feels like you are being watched, you will be more inclined to do the right thing. Doing the right thing in some cases may be difficult. The feeling that others are judging you is always a good motivation.

It is common to find pictures of eyes in places like toilets or public areas. If you have a feeling that you are being watched, it is easy to avoid littering the environment. It also persuades individuals to always clean up after using a public toilet.

If you find this book helpful in anyway a review to support my endeavors is much appreciated.

Dean J. Arquette

The Social Anxiety and Shyness Solution

www.ingramcontent.com/pod-product-compliance
Lightning Source LLC
Chambersburg PA
CBHW031119080526
44587CB00011B/1039